D1536074

HOLY HEADSHOT!
A CELEBRATION OF AMERICA'S UNDISCOVERED TALENT

BY
PATRICK BORELLI & DOUGLAS GORENSTEIN
FOREWORD BY DAVID CROSS

SIMON & SCHUSTER PAPERBACKS
New York London Toronto Sydney

Simon & Schuster Paperbacks
A Division of Simon & Schuster, Inc.
1230 Avenue of the Americas
New York, NY 10020

First Simon & Schuster trade paperback edition October 2008

SIMON & SCHUSTER PAPERBACKS and colophon are registered trademarks
of Simon & Schuster, Inc.

For information about special discounts for bulk purchases,
please contact Simon & Schuster Special Sales at
1-800-456-6798 or business@simonandschuster.com

Manufactured in the United States of America

10 9 8 7 6 5 4 3 2 1

Library of Congress Cataloging-in-Publication Data

Borelli, Patrick, date.
    Holy headshot! : a celebration of America's undiscovered talent / Patrick Borelli and
Douglas Gorenstein.—1st American pbk. ed.
        p.   cm.
    1. Actors—Portraits—Humor. 2. Résumés (Employment)—Humor. I. Gorenstein, Douglas. II. Title.
    PN2095. B67 2008
    791.4302'80973—dc22   2008020557
    ISBN-13: 978–1–4165–9112–2
    ISBN-10:   1–4165–9112–5

HOLY HEADSHOT!

FOREWORD

In life you only get one chance to make a good first impression." That was the tag line of a commercial for underarm deodorant or bread or hip surgery or something—I can't remember what—but that line left me with a good first impression. The statement is true, simply as a matter of physics, I suppose, but worth noting nonetheless. And what could be a better example of this maxim than the modern-day "headshot"? Back in the heady days of the theater (before television and the wireless), lithographs were used for what we call headshots. These were *very* expensive to produce and thus ensured that only rich, snooty, Ivy League dandies would ever tread the boards of the Great White Way.* Then when cheap photography and mass photocopying came along, any idiot with a camera and an index finger could take a picture of any other idiot with four hundred bucks and a misguided dream and, "voilà" (!), as the French would say, instant headshot.

The headshot is the beginning of the process. It is used to immediately weed the chaff from the wheat. When casting directors are working with a director, the first thing they do is send over the headshots of the actors they've selected for consideration. Then the bones thrown, the phrase chanted, and the chicken blood drunk. And then and only then is the spell cast. But first, it's the headshot.

How do you think that any of the greats were cast for their roles? Daniel Day-Lewis in *There Will Be Blood* was cast by Paul Thomas Anderson on the strength of his multiposed headshot wherein he showed his range by setting himself as a doctor, a sexy businessman, a 1950s-like tough guy, and a thoughtful construction worker. Meryl Streep was cast in *Sophie's Choice* once the director saw the headshot wherein she was wearing what looked like a prom gown, sucking on a lollipop, and making "crazy eyes."

In sum, I write the above to alert you to the process. My fear is that without it one would view the following contents of this book with smug condescension. The headshots as little more than the sad products of deluded people to be laughed at.

---

* The term for Canadian Theater.

1

Please don't do this. These are the stars (or at least the working actors) of tomorrow. *They* get it! They know how to best get seen, respected, considered, and, ultimately, work on the silver screen (the Golden screen being reserved for Blu-ray). These people have a crushless dream!!!

—*David Cross*

INTRODUCTION

Thanks for reading *Holy Headshot!* Well, thanks for looking at a bunch of awesome headshots and résumés. Guess how many headshots we looked at to put this book together? Five hundred? One thousand? Nope. Five thousand? Wrong again. Try *fifty* thousand. That's right, fifty plus three zeroes. Seems like a lot but when we first started working on putting the book together, we figured the odds would be that one out of every ten headshots would knock us off our feet. But after flipping through the first hundred headshots, we discovered we only had one, maybe two, that stood out. We realized we had our work cut out for us. And like a fishing boat that's had a little bit of luck, we decided to stay out at sea a tad longer, hoping that somewhere out there, we'd come across the big catch that would reel in dozens of amazing, offbeat headshots. So we posted ads in acting publications in New York, Los Angeles, and Chicago. Then we expanded to ads all over the United States. We visited friends who do casting for late night TV shows and comedy networks in New York. They were kind enough to open their filing cabinets to us, and we took full advantage. Our search went on for over a year. And finally, after all the work and all the searching, what we started to see, when we went back through our collection, was our book. We never did hit that one sweet spot in the vast sea of headshots. We just kept reeling them in, one by one. Ninety-nine percent were tossed back into the ocean. This 1 percent that you hold in your hands represents the big catch. Catching a minnow is no big deal (sorry, John D Bair, p. 126), but reeling in a Yenz Von Tilborg (p. 54), or a Roxie Thomas (p. 90) . . . now that's a fish story worth telling.

What we love about this collection is that no matter how many times we look through it, we always discover something new. It might be a small, subtle detail hidden in a headshot (Loudovikos Hertz, p. 210) or an oddly brazen statement buried in a résumé (Mr. Greeber, p. 136). We've spent a lot of figurative time with the folks in this book, and we've gleaned some valuable lessons we'd like to pass on about how to get noticed, whether you're a fledgling performer or just looking for an office job. Please use the following lessons as a reader's guide so you, too, can comb through these headshots and résumés with the razor-sharp perception of a seasoned casting director.

Should you be an actual casting director who's interested in contacting and actor from this book, there is an email directory at the back.

LESSON #1: DO WHATEVER IT TAKES TO GET NOTICED.

Forty-eight thousand eight hundred ninety-seven headshots were rejected for this book because most were of an affable person, sporting a ho-hum expression and a blasé outfit. Never follow the masses. Instead, try some of the moves employed by the true individuals who made the final cut. The following are useful tactics:

* *Switch genders.* Throw on a wig or a dress and pretend you're a member of the opposite sex.

* *Burnish a weapon and carry it with confidence.* This lets prospective employers know that you mean business and that you own your own weapons and are willing to supply them for use in a violent performance.

* *Don't be afraid to experiment with color.* If you have a favorite color, by all means, use it everywhere and market it as your signature style. No dye job or tattoo display is too overblown.

LESSON #2: CREDITS—AND WE MEAN ALL CREDITS—ARE MARKETABLE.

Be sure to list every single credit that you've ever had. Highlighting that you played Boo Boo the Kitty in your kindergarten play illustrates your long-standing commitment to your craft. If you don't have enough room to list everything, try adding a second or third page, or showing a partial list and state that additional credits are "available upon request." Those three words tell casting directors, "I've done *so* much work that I can't even begin to list it. You'll have to make a special request for it." This maneuver will create the impression that you have a second, private résumé, full of interesting information that only a select group of requesters are privy to.

LESSON #3: LET'S GET PERSONAL.

Every résumé how-to book will advise against getting too personal on a résumé. But that advice is unashamedly for dummies anyway, and we think it's so pre-*American Idol.*

Genuine personality is in the details, so reveal a confidence that you've never told your spouse or therapist. This will grab the reader's attention, and that's what you are hoping to accomplish. Revealing that you are double-jointed and have a third nipple, for example, will definitely get you noticed. Note: Actor Mark Wahlberg revealed he has a third nipple and look how far it has gotten him.

LESSON #4: DRESS FOR THE ROLE YOU WANT, NOT THE ROLE YOU HAVE. (PROPS ARE YOUR FRIENDS!)

You've already landed the role of the unemployed actor. Why should your headshot reveal that? If you want to get a part playing a nun or a cop, go to a costume shop, buy the costume, and have your headshot taken as a nun and a cop. You'll find yourself on *Law & Order* in no time. When it comes to props, a few savvy casting directors will assume that you know how to use a phone, hold a cup, or look at a book. But not every casting director is so insightful. Make sure they know exactly what you're capable of doing by clearly demonstrating your ability to carry a suitcase, swing a racket, or wear a hat.

LESSON #5: LOOK TO THE FUTURE—IT'S NOT ABOUT WHERE YOU'VE BEEN, BUT WHERE YOU'RE HEADED.

A winning résumé lists your past accomplishments and hints at how great you'll be in the future. If you have yet to act in a film but want directors to know you'd consider the job, type "FILM" on your résumé and leave a blank space underneath. This tactic will inspire imagination in casting directors' minds, leaving little opportunity for typecasting, allowing them to envision your potential range regardless of prior experience. Most résumé experts tell you to glowingly focus on past accomplishments. But why not speculate on how good you'd be if only you had some? Confident speculation shows aplomb and a willingness to focus on an objective, and those are traits any employer would be glad to have on board.

LESSON #6: SPECIAL SKILLS WILL THRILL.

If you've got them, flaunt them! Don't be afraid to list every possible thing you can do, no matter how mundane. No skill is too common. Proficient at driving a car? Capable of being fully ambulatory? Do you know how to stare? The more skills you list, the more you will appear to be a genius. And you never know when a casting director will be looking for that one person who can confidently say, "I can fart 'The Star-Spangled Banner.'" After all, rumor has it that the great Marlon Brando got his big break because he could open a beer bottle with his ass.

LESSON #7: SEX IT UP, SEX IT DOWN.

Whether you have pecks like Brad Pitt or moobs like Michael Moore, never underestimate the power of showing some skin. You're probably thinking, "But won't that make me look like a tart? Or desperate?" Not if you do it right. Wearing your favorite bikini (well, if you're a woman) or those old jeans (with no top) lets a casting director know that you are confident about your body. And a confident actor is a working actor.

On the flip side, sometimes it might be a good strategy to eliminate the sex factor as much as possible. How do you do that? Start by not showering. Don't brush your teeth. If you have dirt on your face or hands, leave it. Throw out your razor blades. Wear modest, bland clothing that doesn't match and that covers most of your body. Don't smile or make strong eye contact with the camera. When the photographer snaps the picture, think about an upsetting secret that only you know. And once you get your headshot from the photographer, definitely do not enhance the photo with Photoshop. No teeth whitening. No removal of crow's-feet or laugh lines. No brightening of the skin. Almost every actor is afraid to be seen in their worst state, which is *exactly* why you should be seen that way. You'll stand out from all the airbrushed, fake-smiling, squeaky-clean nobodies.

LESSON #8: SPELL CHECKS ARE UNNECESSARY AND FONTS ARE YOUR FRIENDS.

Nowadays anyone can have a perfectly spelled, grammatically correct résumé. Be a pioneer! Do the opposite and see howe peeple take knowtice. Also, fonts like Helvetica, Times New Roman, and Century scream, "I'm boring and unimaginative." In other words, "I'm only good enough to do extra work." Separate yourself from the millions of other actors using tired, old lettering by choosing the most distracting, obscure fonts like **CHEAP MOTEL**, NEPTUNE, **House of Terror**, and HAMBURGER. Even if your résumé is unreadable, this will show them that you are interested in hard-to-read typography, which implies you are artsy, which might lead them to think you can act. It's a risk worth taking.

LESSON #9: DARE TO COMPARE.

Whether you look remotely like a celebrity, nothing like a celebrity, or are the spitting image of Julia Roberts, it is in your best interest to draw a comparison between you and a particular famous actor. Movie studios may very well prefer to save millions of dollars by hiring someone who *looks* like a movie star, as opposed to hiring the actual star for much more money. So, if you've got a mole on your cheek, bill yourself as the next Robert De Niro. Or lift something heavy in your headshot to instantly draw a comparison between you and action heroes like Sylvester Stallone and Arnold Schwarzenegger. Go on and let them know who you really are directly in your résumé: "I'm a Sandra Bullock type!" Or, "I'm a like a young Steven Seagal." Or, "A lot of people tell me I remind them of Tom Hanks, but only from the movie *Cast Away*." Remember, the more you say it, the more others will believe it.

LESSON #10: CONTINUITY, REPETITION, AND EMOTIONAL RANGE.

Continuity and Repetition

When making a movie, it is essential that an actor be able to repeat the scene exactly the same way over and over again or risk being fired. On a set, this ability to repeat an action is known as continuity. That's why we recommend that you put together a headshot using multiple photos of yourself wearing the same outfit and making the same expression. This may seem redundant, but that's the point. What seems like a lack of creativity on your part is actually the mark of a true professional who can deliver the goods. Take after take after take.

Emotional Range

The other direction to go in is to showcase your ability to emote. How does an actor show emotional range in a headshot? Easy—by making faces. Some of the best headshots contain dozens of tiny photos of the actor in various stages of feeling. From frowning to open-mouthed excitement. From a clench-jawed rage to a squinty-eyed skepticism, a knowing smirk, a wide-eyed hysteria, or even a simple cry—we could go on and on, but you get the point. Acting icon Bette Davis once said, "Good actors I've worked with started out making faces in the mirror, and you keep making faces all your life." Unfortunately, Ms. Davis is now dead and can no longer make faces.

Kitten Kay Sera

Kitten Kay Sera

With Miss Kisses
SAG eligible

kittenandkisses.com

Height: 5'4"
Weight: 120lbs
Hair: Blonde
Eyes: Blue

COMMERCIAL
Vytorin

Principle/National
Pink Lady with Pink Dog

Merck

TELEVISION
Off The Leash

Principle Lead/National Reality Series
With Miss Kisses

Lifetime Television

Dog Whisperer

Kitten gets tips from Cesar Millan for
Miss Kisses

National Geographic

Open Call

Kitten receives her own reality TV show
from the TV Guide Channel

TV Guide

Totally Obsessed

Documentary/Comedy on Kitten's 20 year
obsession with the color pink

VH-1

Blind Date

Producers wanted a Doris Day type
Kitten was chosen to be "set-up"

UPN

Explosive

The Pink Lady Documentary

RTL – Germany

The Kitten and Kisses Show

Reality/Talk show

Youtube.com

Extra

Special Guest Reporter/Host

NBC

NATIONAL PRESS
Access Hollywood
Extreme Hollywood
Reality Chat

Interview with Maria Menounos
Interview
Interview

NBC
E entertainment
TV Guide

KITTEN'S DISCOGRAPHY
Hush The Drama - 1994
Freak On In – 1996
From Box To Beautiful...In Seconds – 2003 featuring Beyonce Knowles on the single "Sex Kitten"

TRAINING
David White Acting Workshop   – Los Angeles

SPECIAL NOTE*******
Kitten's career is based around the color pink. She privately and commercially will ONLY wear pink

9

JOE PASCA

Joseph A. Pasca

Height: 5'1"
Weight: 135
Hair: Black
Eyes: Brown

Film & Television

Toi and Poochie	George	Illuminare Ent.
Olive Juice	Bartender	Doubble Troubble
Good Friday	Skippy	SR Productions
The Rosie O'Donnell Show	Character Performer	Warner Bros. TV
Young Musicians Special	Character Performer	Disney Channel

Stage

Fantasmic!	Character Performer	WDW
Beauty & the Beast	Character Performer	WDW
A Christmas Fantasy	Character Performer	Disneyland
Cartoon Circus	Character Performer	Isl. Of Adventure

Special Skills

New York Accent, Basketball, Football, Golf, Bowling, Play The Drums, Moderate Singer, Moderate Dancer, Basic Puppetry, Bartending Skills

Heigth 5.10 Weigth 165

Aftra-Sag

OSCAR SAUL TEVEZ

OSCAR S.TEVEZ

AFTRA - SAG   Heigth:5'10.Weight:160.

NEW YORK CITY

STAGE

THE RED DEVIL	Red	The Samuel Beckett Theatre. NYC
HEART OF DARKNESS	Doctor	American Theatre Academy. NYC
YA VIENE PANCHO VILLA!	Pancho Villa	Latin american Theatre Festival, at
(Here comes Pancho Villa!)		Teatro Pregones, The Bronx, NYC
THE MAGIC OF ACTING	Workshop	Theatre Works .NYC
GIVE US THIS DAY	Reverend Luis	Village Gate. NYC
INSTANT KARMA	Frank	Wings Theatre NYC
THE BIG LAGOON	Land Owner	Teatro Nacional, EL SALVADOR
INDEPENDENCE DAY	student	Teatro Nacional, EL SALVADOR
THE WARRIOR ANT	Singer	Brooklyn Academy of Music(BAM) NYC
MOTHER COURAGE AND HER CHILDREN	Soldier	Thetre Studio.NYC
THE LAND OF THE DRAGON	Covet Spring	World Children Theatre.NYC
THE LAST WHITE CAB DRIVER	Cesar Medera	Thetre 22 NYC

TELEVISION/FILM

A Day with a dillusional ----   Arnold --- Two Socks productions--NY

Blood Money ---   Chico --- Blood Money productions   ------   NY

THE GUERILLAS--   Lead------   TEMPLE

"OZ" ------   Principal -------   HBO

LATE NITE WITH CONAN OBRIEN   ---   Window washer   --   NBC

"R-XMAS"   ---- -   Gypsi Driver -- Directed by Abel Ferrara.   Valence Films

SPIN CITY ---   Undercover --   ABC

LATE SHOW WITH DAVID LETTERMAN --   Singing Cook   -- CBS

THE COSBY SHOW --   Principal   --   CBS

BIRDS OF PASSAGE   --   Co-Starring   - Les Films Du Triangle,FRANCE

TRAMPS   --   Cook,Supporting   Les Films Du Triangle and WDR.GERMANY

ALL MY CHIDREN   ---   Principal   --   ABC

ONE LIFE TO LIVE   ---   Under Five   ----   ABC

GLORIA ---   Pawnbroker --   Gloria Productions

THE JUROR   --   Mayan shooter   --   Universal

HAPPY NEW YORK   --   The cuban   --   VILM Productio. POLAND

POISON-- (Grand Prize at Sundance)--- Todd Haynes Directed.   Bronce Eye Prod.

THE IMAGICAL JOURNEY--   Shaman   Rock People Productions.NYC

THE STONE   ----   Lead   ---   Independent Prod.

MANHATTAN BRIDGE----   Day Player -----   Hiro Productions.

TRAINING- National School of the Arts , HB Studio NYC. SKILL :Spanish Dialects,basic
French and Ittalian.Martial Arts,Sketch Artist,Culinary Training.Excelent Hands,Singer
and Dancer.VIDEO CD AVAILABLE ON REQUEST.

Sybil Presley
"The Tennessee Stressbuster"

Sybil Presley

www.sybilpresley.com

Height: 5'8"   Weight: 150lbs.   Eyes: Brown   Hair: Brown   Age: 60

Talents:

Actress, Model, Comedienne, Poet, Author, Writer, Voice Overs

Video Credits:

The Girls All Get Prettier at Closing Time – Mickey Gilley
Something Like That – Dolly Pardon
Friends in Low Places – Garth Brooks

Movie Credits:

Love Leads the Way – Walt Disney
Sweet Dreams – The Patsy Cline Story
Hair
The Attica Prison Story
Marie
The Hank Williams Story
What Comes Around
Concrete Cowboy
Living Proof
The Road to Graceland
Walk the Line
Southern Comfort
Take Me Back to Beale
From Normal to Oily
My Blueberry Nights

Television Credits:

The Ralph Emery Show – WSM Nashville
Nite Owl Theatre – Guest Host, WKRN Nashville
Dot Moore/Gulfcoast Today – WALA Mobile
You Can Be a Star – WSM Nashville
Good Morning Memphis – Fox Channel 13 Memphis
Alive at Nine – Channel 3 News Memphis
American Idol
Local Newscasts
National Networks: CNN, ABC, NBC, BBC

Films and Documentaries Worldwide

Stage:

The Memphis Idol Play – New Daisy Theatre Memphis

Festivals:

Memphis Music & Heritage Festival,
by Center for Southern Folklore

JOHN WEIGAND

JOHN WEIGAND
AFTRA SAG EMC

Height: 5'6" **Hair:** Salt & Pepper **Weight:** 160 lbs. **Eyes:** Blue-Green
Bari-Tenor (Low F to High G)

THEATRE
New York

The Golem of Gavah (AEA Reading)	Mr. Holtzman, Community Leader	American Center
Glory, Glory Hallelujah!	Dick Cheney/Ben Franklin	Theater for the New City
Fiorello! (with Tony LoBianco)	Judge Carter /Ed Peterson	Snug Harbor Music Hall
Extra Innings (Reading)	Ernie/Stanley	Lambs Theatre
It's Beginning To Look A Lot Like Murder	Quincy	Daryl Roth2
The Most Happy Fella	Doc	Acorn Theatre at Theatre Row

National Tour

Fiddler on the Roof	Avram, The Bookseller	Troika Entertainment

Regional

Around the World in 80 Days	Ralph/Mandiboy	Fulton Theatre, PA
The Mousetrap	Major Metcalf	Fulton Theatre, PA
My Fair Lady	Colonel Pickering	Dutch Apple Dinner Theatre, PA
Beauty and the Beast	Maurice	Broadway Palm Dinner Theatre, AZ
The Diary of Anne Frank	Dussel	Jenny Wiley Theatre, KY
Show Boat	Captain Andy	La Comedia Dinner Theatre, OH

TELEVISION (U/5's)

As The World Turns	Mr. White	CBS
All My Children	The Waiter Who Looks Like Janet	ABC
Chappelle's Show	Dr. Phil	Comedy Central

FILM

The Standard Man	Santa	Bozymowski & Cody Indie Film
Spectropia	William van Alen	Toni Dove
The Kiss	William LeMessurier	Bozymowski & Cody Indie Film

TRAINING (Wynn Handman, HB, Michael Howard, T. Schreiber, Times Squares Dance Studios, Northwestern University, BSJ, MSJ)

Acting	Michael Becket
Scene Study	Wynn Handman, Terry Schreiber
Audition Technique	Arnold Mungioli, Caryn West
Comedy Improv	Alan Arkin
Speech	Chuck Guajardo
Singing (Bari-Tenor: Low F to High G)	David Brunetti, Alan Bowers
Dance (Jazz)	Nikki Harris

Special Skills

Athletics	Weightlifting
Dance	Jazz, Disco, Polka, Square Dance, Waltz
Dialects	Authentic New Orleans Accent, British
Other	Former Corp VP, USN Lt., Salesman, Teacher, Driver (Auto), Passport

Roberto Lombardi

Roberto Lombardi

Height: *6 feet*
Weight: *165*
Age Range: *32 - 45*
Physique: *Athletic / Muscular*
Hair Color: *Brown*
Eyes: *Blue*

> Teleprompter
> Medical Terminology

Film

Mya	Lead	Rob Hawk Productions / Rob Hawk
Just Like Me	Lead	Rob Hawk Productions / Rob Hawk
vOosHa dAy	Principal	Rob Hawk Productions / Rob Hawk
The Dig	Supporting	3 Point Production Group / Thad Reid
Bazookas: The Movie	Supporting	Truancy Films / Michael G. Leonard
Shooter	Featured	Paramount Pictures / Antoine Fuqua
True Crime	Supporting	Star Films / Katie Selyanina
Framework	Featured	Partners In Krime Productions / Kathy Grasso
An Unexplained Murder	Lead	One Light Films / Jamie Mengual
If You Could Say It In Words	Featured	A Chip & A Chair Films / Nicholas Gray
Our Business	Principal	Fretboard Pictures / John Rhee
Eddie And The Cruisers	Featured	MGM / Martin Davidson
Final Showing	Lead	Past & Present Productions / Frank Jacobs
Blow Out	Featured	MGM / Brian DePalma
The Main Course	Supporting	Past & Present Productions / Frank Jacobs

Television

Parco P.I.	Featured	Court TV / Tom Bell
Tucci Live	Guest Star	MCTV Channel "J" / Lin Tucci

Commercials

Engineering An Empire	Featured	The History Channel / Film Rite Entertainment
PSA - NCADD: 'Father's Choice'	Lead	Fretboard Pictures / John Rhee

Industrial

Covenant Security Service	Lead	Benji Bakshi Productions / Jim McGinty

Theater

Grease	Principal	Art Theater Group
Godspell	Principal	Art Theater Group
Dames At Sea	Featured	AJC Players / Tony Costandino
Inherit The Wind	Supporting	AJC Players / Tony Costandino

Training
Film Acting: Philadelphia, Pa., *Mike Lemon Casting*
Law EnforcementTraining Center: Brunswick, Ga., *U.S. Department of Homeland Security*
Scarpell School Of Singing: Warminster, Pa., Advanced Vocal, *Debbie Scarpell*
Temple University, Philadelphia, Pa.: Basic Acting, Drama, Comedy & Movement

Performer Skills
Spoken Languages: Italian, Spanish (not fluent).
Athletic Skills: Baseball, Track & Field, Swimming, Cycling, Bowling, Weight Lifting.
Accents: Italian, Southern, Spanish, British, New York (Bronx), Australian.
Musical Instruments: Drums, Bass Guitar, Percussion, Keyboards, Guitar.
Professional Musician with over ten albums recorded and hundreds of concert performances
Songwriter with over 300 copyrights.
Singing Voice: Tenor, Baritone.
Trained Law Enforcement Agent with over 10 years experience. Firearms & Defensive Tactics qualified.

Shelley Krawch

SHELLEY M. KRAWCHUK - SAG Eligible

Race: Caucasian / Eastern European   **Hair:** Brown-Red   **Eyes:** Blue
                                                     Height: 155   **Weight:** 5' 10"

Film

Metamorphosis	Principle - The Woman	Propeller – USA Productions
Welcome to Hawaii	Co-Star – Wife	Bao Nguyen Productions
Home Again – HIFF 2007	Principle - Casting Agent	Creative Media Productions
Soul Savior	Co-Star - Angel	Ventureway Productions
Two Sides of the Same Coin	Principle - Wife	Karp Productions
Part-time Ninja	Co-Starring	Digital Productions
It's About Time	Co-starring	D & N Productions
A Clearing in the Woods	Principle-Virginia	Wayne Ward Productions
The Presidents' Son	Co-Star – First Lady	HPR Video 2 Productions

WEB

Honolulu's China Town	Web Travel Host	Justin Weiler Productions

Theater – Stage

Comedy Crusaders	Improvisation Troupe	Ongoing Performances
Jasmina and the Janshir	Lead - Sorceress	Amara-Kismet Productions

Industrial

Aloha United Way	*Principle- Drug Addict*	*Kinetic Productions*

Commercials

List available upon request

Training

Commercial Workshop	Anna Fishburne	Audition Techniques	Margaret Doversola
Cold Read	Joji Yoshida	Improvisation	Joji Yoshida
Acting for the Camera	Wayne Ward	Advanced Performance	Wayne Ward
Meisner Technique	Don Owen		

Voice/Diction

Dr. Lois Weis	University of Hawaii

Special Skills

Accents: British, Southern United Stated, East Coast United States, French, Canadian and more.
Languages: Studying Italian, French four-year study.
Physical/Sports: Sailing – racing sloop, Hiking, Backpacking, camping, bicycling, kayaking, boogie-boarding, water aerobics, Bocci, darts, shoot 22 rifle and shotgun, fishing, crabbing, clamming, and shrimping (home-made traps).
Music: Classical Piano, Bassoon, Church choir – alto, Country Western vocalist
Licenses / Certifications: Legal Nurse Consultant, Registered Nurse, Oncology Certification
Miscellaneous: Gourmet cook, Wine Club founder, Bartender, Animal rescue,
Fine art sales representative, Teak and wood refinisher, Faux finishing, Horticulture
Citizenship: Canadian citizen, and United States citizen

RAY SEIDEN

Ray Seiden
SAG / AFTRA

Height: 6'0"   Hair: Brown
Weight: 200 lbs.   Eyes: Brown

Film

Film	Principal Roles	Directors
INVITATION TO A SUICIDE	Cop #3	Loren Marsh
HOT ICE	EMT	John Bianco
MARCI X	Correction Officer Dorset	Richard Benjamin
KATE AND LEOPOLD	Sanitation Worker	James Mangold
THOMAS CROWN AFFAIR	Officer Houser	John McTiernan
SWEET'N'LOWDOWN	Pool Player	Woody Allen
THE YARDS	Officer Osbourne	James Gray
BELLY	Omaha, Neb. Cop-Stunt	Hype Williams
PICTURE PERFECT	Nick's Friend	Glenn Gordon Caron
PI	Transit Cop	Darren Aronofsky
TO WONG FOO	Transvestite	Beeban Kidron
TOXIC AVENGER, PART 2&3	Dogman	Kaufman / Herz

Television

MAURY POVICH SHOW	Peeping Tom	Mopo Prod., Inc.
IN DA KHUT	James	Rudely St. Eloi
WHEN I GROW UP	Cop #1	Vince Misiano
WWF PROMO	Biplane pilot	Meteor Productions
ALIENS IN THE FAMILY	Alien Warlord	Tom Trbovich

Theatre / Voice Overs

WHO KILLED ORSON WELLES	The Waiter	Lee Linkous
THE LONG ISLAND FILM FESTIVAL		Voice Over
ONE FLEW OVER THE CUCKOO'S NEST	Ruckly	Express Theatre Group
IRON-TEK ADVANCED PERFORMANCE NUTRITION		Voice Over

Commercials / Industrials   (principal roles)   List Upon Request

Training

Lynn Winters' Studio	Scene Study
Stanley Greene Media Training Center	Voice Overs
National Model United Nations	Public Speaking
Dan Duckworth Private Coaching	Voice Overs
Queens College	Scene study
AQP theatre workshop	Acting Technique

Special Skills / Experiences

Body-building, Martial Arts, Aviation, Double-jointed, Music, guitar

Own: Full Police, Guard, EMT Uniforms, Court Officer, Tuxedo, Karate Gi, Priest, Drag Outfit

ALBERT TYLER

Acting Resume

Schools

Performer's Academy   Acting   Laguna, Ca.   2/2007-present   Barbizon School of modeling   Modeling   Anaheim, Ca. 6/1999-12/1999   Barbizon School of modeling   Acting   Stratford, Ca. 1/1993-6/1993

Movie Parts

O.J. Simpson Murder Case	Detective	Movie extra	1993
Quick	Football Coach	Movie extra	1993
Pepsi Cola Commercial	In Crowd	Movie extra	1993
Graduation	Escort	Movie extra	1993

Skills

Ex Football Player   6'-2" solid 305lbs.
Ex Professional Wrestler
Some Boxing
Body Builder

Employment

Designer-   Nuclear Power Plant   Southern Edison   San Clemente, Ca.

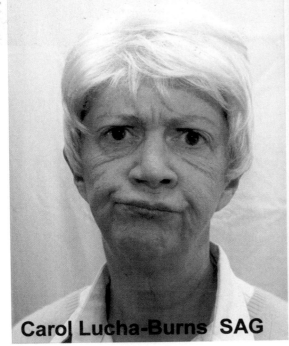

Carol Lucha-Burns SAG

CAROL BURNS
SAG - AEA

Performing (representative of my current age)

Pippin	Granny
Lettice and Lovage	Lettice
Annie	Miss Hannigan
The Importance of Being Earnest	Lady Bracknell
Anything Goes	Mrs. Harcourt
The House of Bernarda Alba	Prudencia
A Funny Thing…	Domina
Jerry's Girls	Various

Industrials and Club Work in Japan

USA 100- Atami Resorts, Japan	*American Club, Tokyo*
Hilton Starhill Supper Club, Tokyo	*Camp Zama, and various military bases in Japan*

From 1965-69 I performed in Tokyo, made some television appearances, and did voice over work. From 1969 to the present I have focused on college teaching with a few theatre performances when scheduling permitted. Recent retirement gives me free time for TV, film and print work.

Film Background Performer

Disney's Underdog	Photographer
Gone Baby Gone	Mourner
21	Shopper
27 Dresses	Wedding Guest
The Women	Anxious mother

Specialties

Drive a 2006 bright blue mini-cooper S convertible, standard shift, limited (but pathetically rusty) Japanese, eccentric dancing-tap , kick-boxing, excellent mimic with a good ear for dialects, foil fencing, puppeteer. Amiable, patient, reliable, and great with kids and curmudgeons.

Education and Training

Syracuse University –Drama and Sociology
Acting-Sandy Meisner
Musical Theatre-Lehman Engel
Classics-Philip Burton
Jazz-Hanya Holm
Tap-Jerry Ames

Eric Gipson

Eric Gipson
SAG E

Height--5'7"; Weight--140; Hair--Brown; Eyes--Brown

Film

Beyond A Reasonable-Principle /Doubt / Alan /Peter Hyams
. Blonde Ambition-Supporting/Window Washer/Scott Marshall
Control Your Roll—Principal/Host (LSUHSC childhood obesity series)
The Year Without Santa Claus/ Supporting/Power Elf/ Ron Underwood
Mr. Brooks—Featured/Alcoholic/Bruce A Evans
The Ray of Sunshine/Principal/District Attorney /BPCC
These Days—Supporting/Bar employee / Tricom
The Ruffian—Featured/Reporter /ESPN
Factory Girl/Featured/Taxi driver /George Hickenlooper

Television

"Mad Scientist"—Live TV appearances throughout Southern U.S. for Shreveport's Sci-Port Discovery Center.
   Segments include comedic improvisation with news anchors.
Mad Scientist Ball commercials: as Groucho Marx (2001) and Rod Serling (2003)
Houser Shoes commercials, North and South Carolina, role of father/husband

Theater Productions

Asheville, NC: *Lone Star, Move Over Mrs. Markham, Rats, Greetings, The Odd Couple*;
New Orleans: *Room Service, Unforgettable, A Midsummer Night's Dream, Lo and Behold!, A Typical Conversation in a Chinese Restaurant, The Voices of New Orleans, The Shakespeare Murders*
Shreveport: *Play it Again Sam*

Comedy and Performance Art   Available upon request

Emcee (recent)

Gonzo Art Show, Shreveport—host, *Shaking the Tree*, Port Belly Project performance at Shreveport Regional Council
   ArtSpace--emcee/Whirling Dervish
ArtScare, Shreveport Regional Arts Council—emcee and Zoltar the Great
Krewe of Barkus & Meoux Ball—Co-emcee

Voiceover

All Access IMAX TV commercial for Sci-Port Discovery Center, Shreveport
Asheville, NC Board of Realtors *Share the Warmth* TV commercial

Unique Talents   Capable of all genres, including professional, intellectual, crazy, white and blue collar Multiple voice and accents, including: TV/radio broadcaster, extreme rapid-fire, all U.S. regions, and many foreign. Strong with impersonations. Basic voice is non-regional.

Elastic face with multiple expressions, eyeball wiggling, tumbling and falling, can snap fingers off anything, guitar, some piano, can verbally reproduce most cartoon noises
Some Spanish and German

Education B.A. in Communications-Journalism, Louisiana State University, Shreveport, LA Acting workshops in New Orleans, Shreveport and Asheville, NC

SKIPPY "D"

SKIPPY "D"

	Height: 5' 6"	Hair: Blonde
	Weight: 137	Eyes: Blue

S.A.G.

FILM

"The Ministers"	Cameraman	The Ministers, LLC
"Multiple Sarcasms"	Car Driver w/Antique Cadillac	
"The Brave One"	Perpatrator	Redemption Pictures
"Illegal Tender"	Car Driver w/Antique Cadillac	Crumk / Spike Lee/John Singleton
"Pride & Glory"	Car Driver w/Oldsmobile /Street Thug	Avery Pix
"Enchanted"	Country Boy Filming Sights	Andalasia / Disney
"Tenderness"	Car Driver / Country Boy/Biker	Upstate Pix
"Across The Universe"	60's Biker	Period Musical Inc. / Julie Taymor
"Stunt Seven"	Boat Driver	Hal Needham
"The Tourist"	Camera Guy	Axium Visual
"Watching The Detectives"	Tough Guy	Axium Visual
"Analyze That"	Prison Biker / Inmate	Harold Ramos
"The River of Copsa Mica"	Vladamir / Featured	Radius 5 Media / Dustin Highbridge
"In The Hood"	Roping Cowboy	Snygg Brothers
"Gone With The Wieners"	Jake / Featured and Assistant Producer	Mark Leland/C.A.T. Productions
"Pergatory Blues"	Farmer "Bubba" / Featured	El Cinema
"Monday Night Mahem"	Extra/Preferred Roles & ABC Technician	ABC / John Tatturo
"In The Cut"	Business Owner	Meg Ryan
"Gunmen"	Drago-Henchman/ATV & Fight Stunts	Evan / Image Factory

FEATURED COMMERCIALS

"Slomin's Shield"	Pirate / First Mate	North East Regional
"Rock Band Band" Rock Band Band Video Game	Road Manager / Roadie / Featured	Bex Schwartz VH1/MTV Networks
"Shootout at the D&T Corral"	Ernst & Young (Ernst & Stunts)	Joe Daley-Miles Assoc., Inc.
"ESPN Sports Center / Beck's Beer"	Skippy "D" as Skippy "D"	John Doran - ESPN Sports
"Coke Zero"	Danger Dan / Principal Player	Jordan Brady/ Preston Lee/Area 51
"GMC Trucks"	Danger Dan / Principal Player	Jordan Brady/Preston Lee/Area 51
"White Chocolate Kit Kat Bar" - Hershey	Biker "Skippy D" / Principal Player	Radical Media / National
"Motorcycle Mike & Danger Dan" Promo for Slammin' Saturday / SPIKE TV	Danger Dan / Principal Player	Chris Weinstein / Canned Films

TELEVISION

"Damages"	Homeless Guy	TBS
30 Rock	Deer Hunter	NBC
Law and Order - SVU	Perpatrator	NBC Universal
Law and Order - CI	North Carolina Redneck	NBC Universal
Six Degrees	Street Tough w/5.0 Mustang	Touchtone Pics
The Black Donnelleys	Pool Player	NBC Universal
"Gun Fighters"	Re-enactor	History
"Third Watch"	Rally Player	CBS
"SPIKE TV - Daredevil Reunion"	Danger Dan	Canned Films
Knights of Prosperity / AKA I Robbed Mick Jagger	Coney Island Cowboy	

STAGE

"House Of Blue Leaves"	Arty O'Shaughnessy	Off Off Broadway-NY
"Lone Star"	Ray	Off Off Broadway-NY
"Legends Of The West"	Wild Bill Hickock	Keane University Theater-NJ
"Doc Skinum Snake Oil Salesman"	Sheriff	Keane University Theater-NJ

NATIONAL / REGIONAL TOURS

"Wild Bill Hickock Re-enactment"	Trick Shooter Guest Appearance	Mark Allen - WWAC
"Black Jack"	Trick Shooter Guest Appearance	Dave Osborne
"Wild West Show"	Bill Hickcock, Trick Shooter, Head Wrangler	Skippy "D" for Horizon Ent.
"Dead Legends"	Father Time / Guns & Knives	Skippy "D"/Craig Neier Entertainment
"The Frontier Riders Wild West Show"	Wild Bill, Curly Bill, Black Jack, Sheriff, Wrangler	Carl Burrows
"Circus With A Purpose"	Wrangler, Emcee, Actor, Pawney Bill	Michael Sandlofer

TRAINING

Acting: CBHS Drama; American Academy of Dramatic Arts - Manhattan, NY

SPECIAL SKILLS:

Professional Cowboy/Rodeo, Motorcycles, ATV's, Marine Craft, Surf, Ski (Snow and Water), Scuba Diver, Singer, Wild West Arts
Specialist and Trainer, Trick Shooter, Firearms Expert, Avid Outdoorsman (Fishing/Hunting). Have cars, trucks, motorcycles, ATV's,
boats, snowmobiles, tractors, etc. - Vehicle and Equipment list available upon request. Extensive wardrobe. Precision Driver and Stunts.

Rainey Welch

Rainey Welch

www.raineywelch.com

Film & Television

GHOST STORY	Lead	Andrew Wood - Director
LOVE SERENADE	Lead	Jose-Luis Orbegozo
THE OFF ISLANDERS	Lead	Andy Ritchie
THE CLOSET DOOR	Lead	Dan Rucker
LOSER	Lead	Alan Hotchman
BAZZINI'S, NOW OPEN LATE	Lead	Zac Stuart-Pontier
SONG FOR CELIA	Lead	Ron Eigen - Eigen Brothers Prod.
FOUR DEAD BATTERIES	Supporting	Hyrem Martinez - Up Past Midnight Prod.
POOL	Lead	Joseph Latimore - Mad Daimoku Prod.
FLIP EM OFF {Pilot}	Sketch Characters	Rob Medaska - Sunset Media Prod.
BREAKING VEGAS	Supporting	History Channel/Atlas Media Corp.

New York Theatre

SCHOOL NIGHT & LIQUID COURAGE	sketch and improvisation	Chris Gethard - Upright Citizens Brigade Theatre
ANTON IN SHOW BUSINESS	Lisabette	Heather Guthrie - Bunyip Theatre Co.
COMPANY "Not Getting Married Today"	Amy	Catherine Gaffigan - New Dance Arts Center
FIVE WOMEN WEARING THE SAME DRESS	Mindy	Heather Guthrie - Bunyip Theatre
BABY WITH THE BATHWATER	Helen	Kyra Simring - SliceofLife Theatre Co.
THE SWISS VILLAGE	Gina	Niki Paluga - Staged Reading
BLITZKRIEG	God	Ron Glucksman - Staged Reading
THE AUTOBIOGRAPHY OF GOD	Melissa	Donovan Dolan - Slice ofLife Theatre Co.
LOS ANGELES THEATRE "LOVE MINUS"	Karla	Bryan Fogel & Sam Wolfson - Stella Adler Theatre

Stand-Up Comedy

Don't Tell Mama, Rose's Turn, Stand-Up New York, The Duplex and Caroline's - New York City

Training

Improvisation	Chris Gethard, Zach Woods, Lennon Parham, & Charlie Saunders (UCB School)
Improvisation Workshop	Ron Riggle (UCB and Saturday Night Live)
Acting Technique/Stanislavski	Catherine Gaffigan (Producer's Club)
Acting Technique/Stanislavski	Black Nexxus -Rotating Faculty
Stand-Up Comedy	Stephen Rosenfield (American Comedy Institute)
Improvisation	Deb Rabbei & Jay Rhoderick (American Comedy Institute)
Cold Reading, Scene Study	Claudia A. Bloom (Private)
Classical/Shakespeare	Ted Zurkowski (Private)
Voice/Singing	Mike Mitchell (Private)
Soap Opera Technique	Eli Tray (TVI Studios)

Education

University of Iowa
M.F.A. in Performance
University of Alabama, B.A.

Special Skills

Hapkido, Kung Fu, Kickboxing, Capoeira, Yoga, Running, Pilates, Weight Training, Aerobics, Swimming, Biking, Horseback Riding, Tennis, Roller Skating, Modern Dance, Hip Hop, Jazz, Ballet, Tap, Swing, Hiking, Hoolahoop, White Water Rafting, Dodgeball, Rubber Face
Dialects: Southern, New York, Midwestern, Russian, British, Cockney

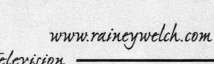

AUTOBIOGRAPHY OF GOD

"tightly dressed sex kitten Melissa, has a native self reflective bent that is right on, when not self deprecating. **Rainey Welch** plays her as a lip pursing, finger curling bundle of orgasm and compassion, the perfect combination of traits for self hating Mel's heavenly salvation."
Larry Litt - New York Theatre Wire

HOLLIS GRANVILLE
SAG & AFTRA

HOLLIS GRANVILLE

SAG • AFTRA

Leading Man	Age Range:	55-65
2nd Leads	Height:	5'9"
Heavy	Weight:	210
Night Club Singer	Voice:	Baritone

MOVIES

TRUST THE MAN	Farm Worker *(Day Player)*	Julianne Moore
DOWN TO EARTH	Sick Man *(Day Player)*	Chris Rock
DEVIL'S ADVOCATE	Homeless - Mugger *(Day Player)*	Al Pacino
REGARDING HENRY	Butler *(Day Player)*	Harrison Ford
COOKIE	Court Officer *(Featured)*	Peter Falk
SHE DEVIL	Court Officer *(Featured)*	Roseanne Barr
SOMEONE ONE ELSE'S AMERICA	Fisherman *(Featured)*	Indie Feature
FRENCH CONNECTION	Cop *(U-5 & Day Player)*	Gene Hackman
FORT APACHE THE BRONX	Witness *(Day Player)*	Paul Newman
STEAL A KISS	Cab Driver *(Day Player)*	Feature Film
PANIC IN NEEDLE PARK	Guard *(Featured)*	Al Pacino
HOSPITAL	Orderly *(Featured)*	George C. Scott

TELEVISION *(Day Player Roles and U-5)*

AS THE WORLD TURNS • ONE LIFE TO LIVE • EDGE OF NIGHT • ANOTHER WORLD
SEARCH FOR TOMORROW • ALL MY CHILDREN • SATURDAY NIGHT LIVE

COMMERCIALS / INDUSTRIAL FILM *(Reel Available ~ No Current Conflicts)*

SUCRETS • AT&T • IRS • SCHAEFER BEER • SUDAFED • KELLOGG'S • UNITED AIRLINES
LIFE SAVERS • CHEMICAL BANK • KRAFT • MINUTE MAID • WESTINGHOUSE • NYNEX
SARA LEE CAKES • BIC LIGHTERS • FORD TRUCKS • TUMS • HERTZ • ROY ROGERS
MYLANTA II • BENDERS CURLERS • TYLENOL

PLAYS

TRIAL OF DR. BECK	Police Officer	Henry Street Settlement
THREE SHADES OF HARLEM	Lead	Roger Furman's New Heritage Repertory Theatre
THE SUPER	Super	Imiri Baraka *(Leroi Jones, dir.)* Black Arts Theatre
EXPERIMENTAL DEATH UNIT #1	Soldier	Imiri Baraka *(Leroi Jones, dir.)* Black Arts Theatre

EDUCATION

Acting - Gene Frankel Theatre Workshop *(Graduate)*
Soap / **On-Camera** - Margo McKee's Soundstage
Voice & Speech - Columbia University *(1 year)*

Complete N.Y.C. Police Sergeant Uniform
Complete N.Y.C. Police Uniform, Own Tuxedo
1989 Toyota Camry available

Stephen Andrew Mayo

Born in Billings Montana, I was raised in a small town called Colstrip, one of those places where everybody knows everybody else. I have been entertaining family, friends and other people as long as I can remember, in whatever ways possible. I have always liked entertaining people whether it was through jokes, performances of stunts. I am inspired by break dancers, stunt men martial artists, and movies ranging from Action through Fantasy and Comedy. Some of my favorite actors include Ewan Mcgreggor, Heath Ledger and Alan Tudyk.

Skills: I'm best known for my physical performance abilities. I am a self taught contortionist specializing in dislocation. Most of these tricks came naturally as a child and have been worked on over the years.

Usual contortions: dislocation and rotation of my shoulders, dislocation of my wrists, dislocation of my hips, extreme flexibility

Experience in Gymnastics, Yoga, Karate, Taekwando, Boxing, Wrestling, and many other activities have added to my physical ability in the areas of contortionism and other stunts.

Other performance experience includes school plays from middle school through high school. I participated in Speech & Drama where I tried almost every event; Humorous solo, humorous duo, original oratory, pantomime, and impromptu.

I was also the drummer for Jazz band in Middle School and Pep Band through High School.

Jennifer Kendall

Jennifer Kendall
Bay Area, California ❧ Los Angeles, California ❧ Orange County, California

Gender: Female
Height: 5 feet 3 inches
Weight: 102
Age Range: 16 - 26
Physique: petite
Hair Color: brown
Hair Length: medium
Eyes: blue
Ethnicity: Caucasian, French, Dutch, Welch
Voice Type: Mezzo-Soprano

Film
Click: Waitress/Extra   Scotty Dugan, Scotty and Dugan Productions

Television
The Man Next Door (TV Movie): Student/Extra   Lamont Johnson

Commercials
Orbitz: Audience   Stasia Bray, MTV Productions
Great America: Participant/Onlooker   Paramount Productions

Theater
The Crucible: Lead Crier   Michael Towers, Westford Academy
Little Shop of Horrors: Ensemble   Michael Towers, Westford Academy
School House Rock: Ensemble   Patrick O'Neil, Palo Alto Children's Theater

Modeling
Fit Model: Rollover Hollywood   San Jose, CA
Fit Model: We Bop Kids   Berkeley, CA

Writing Projects
"Surviving the Joneses" (memoir): Writer   Bay Area, CA: In progress
"Ode to the Strawberry" (poem): Writer   Santa Barbara, CA: Santa Barbara City College
"If Only" (one-act play): Writer & Director   Boston, MA: Westford Academy

Music & Lyrical Background
Vh1 Song Of The Year Competition 2005, 2 time finalist (August & September);
Lyrics-Only Category for 'All In My Head" [August] and
Lyrics-Only Category for "Ending This Before The Pain" [September];
Runner up & Honorable Mention in Lyrics-Only Category [June and July]

Training
Acting Essentials	Los Altos, CA: Foothill College, Gregory Smith
Creative Writing	Santa Barbara, CA: Santa Barbara City College, Susan Jenkins
Advanced Acting	Boston, MA: Phil Valentine, Casting Director
Beginning Acting	Boston, MA: Phil Valentine, Casting Director
Commercial Acting	San Jose, CA: John Robert Powers, Barbara Johnson
Sitcom Acting	San Jose, CA: John Robert Powers, Barbara Johnson

Skills
Athletic Skills: Soccer, Aerobics, Running, Bowling, Swimming, Horseback Riding, Rollerblading, Cycling, Snow Skiing, Cross Country Skiing, Songwriting, Poetry, Singing, Piano
Dance: Club/Freestyle, Hip Hop, Line, Jazz
Accents: Southern, Texan, British

Employment Details
Job Categories: Acting, Modeling, Songwriting, Promotional, Hosting, Performance
Are you willing to work unpaid?: Yes
Authorized to work in United States: Yes

Erin
Douglas
Larson

Erin Douglas Larson

Statistics:
Height: 6'1"
Weight: 178 lbs
Hair: Blonde
Shirt: Medium
Pants: 32 x 34
Suit: 42 long

Television:
Was in the opening scene of a TV pilot named Demea. I played a Priest.
The Bicyclist; TV pilot; to be shown on the internet first.

Commercials:
Prepared and performed a 3 minute commercial at acting school.

Films:
Wicker-Independent film (exemplar films) played a Preacher. Can be viewed at exemplarfilms.com.
A Variation in Action; played an alien that takes on human form. Can be viewed at http://www.vimeo.com/clip:193660
For God and country-to be filmed August 07 (will play a General)

Training:
Acting class; auditioning-Jodi Rothfield
Acting class; commercials.
Acting class; performing monologues.
Acting Class; cold reading techniques.
Acting Workshop; improvisation and to prepare for the Demea shoot.
Acting coach; worked with an acting coach to prepare for an audition.
Modeling classes; John Casablanca's-March – June 2006.
Studied studio recording for 1 year at Evergreen State College; completed several recording projects which included multi-tracking, adding special effects, editing, etc.
Dance Classes; Tango (1978). Performed in the King Dome.
Piano lessons.

Plays/Performance:
Various school and church plays as a youth.
Performed the Tango (with a group of dancers) in the King Dome (1978). I have also sung in many choirs; church and school. I used to perform magic shows as a youth. Performed my own piano compositions for audiences as large as 350 (and as young as 14). Various speaking engagements; both in Spanish English. I also performed various piano pieces (Chopin, etc.) at piano recitals.

Abilities/Skills/Awards:
Good natural acting skills. Here is what one director that I worked with said about my acting ""*viewing the footage only confirmed that you were a great find; your experience shows, and I love the subtle quirks you were able to give to the Alien. You breathed life into that character that I simply hadn't even imagined when I wrote the script. Thank you for being a part of this*".

Speak Fluent Spanish.
Can speak with a Spanish accent.
Sing Bass/Baritone in Choirs.
Body Builder; I have been working out for about 10 ½ years. Was a wrestler in high school (they called me the "little tiger"). I still remember my wresting moves.
Can do various voices-I have performed "Uncle Remus" stories to audiences for years (since I was 12 years old).
Have a natural ability to become the character when acting.
Excellent computer skills; (most Microsoft products, etc.).
Have worked for state government for 17 years, and have learned how to work with well with all types of personalities. I have been a supervisor during many of the years that I have worked for state government.
Intermediate knowledge of music theory .I have composed music on the piano, and can read music at the intermediate level. I passed level 5 music theory with the London School of Music, and level 4 playing the piano.
Graduated with an MBA in Financial Management with a 3.94 GPA.
Have a good knowledge of sports nutrition and supplements that are effective.
Good public speaking skills.

Ray Normandeau

AFTRA & SAG --seeking only: Commercials and skits

Photo: © R Frazier

Ray Normandeau, AFTRA - SAG

Recently did BG work on a

commercial
thru www.BGroundInc.com

More pix and
IMDB credits at
www.RayNYC.us

Raymond B Normandeau

AFTRA # 19177   SAG # 60273

Commercials 2006:
None at press time,
therefore no possible conflicts

Stage Experience:
Retired Carnival Side Show Talker
Guinness Book of World Records Narrator
Magic Show major illusions and MC
Bare Breasted Mermaid Parade MC
Interviewee and interviewer

Trade Shows/Product Demoes:
Game Show Host for Proctor-Silex
Appliance, Food, Electronic, Toy, and Hardware products,
E.G.: Wear-Ever and Cuisinart
Portrayed Swiss Knight Swiss Cheese "Swiss Knight",
making personal appearances in suit of armor speaking with
French accent as tie-in with commercials

Raconteur (story teller/talker) for:
Media events (Radio, TV and Print)
Carnival Side Shows
NY Historical Society
Brooklyn Historical Society
City Lore
Coney Island USA
Museum of the City of New York

Languages:
French is Mother Tongue
Valid Canadian Passport

Wardrobe and Props Owned: *
1 EMT, Ambulance Technician -with equipment

classic white & green with badge OF navy
2 Doctor (ward, office, ER, etc.)
3 NYS Court Room Officer
4 Operating Room Scrub Set (head to toe)
5 Lab Technician
* N.B.: Partner to match, available as above
6 Priest
7 Tuxedo
8 Chef

Specialized Film & TV Experience:

As the French speaking chef with Susan Sarandon and
Willem Dafoe in
    "Light Sleeper"
                    NOW IN VIDEO STORES

Ambulance Paramedic / EMT or Doctor in;
        "NYPD Blue", etc., etc.

Medical Examiner in;
        "America's Most Wanted", etc.

Nerd with thick glasses and plaid shirt in;
    Various Commercials, TV and film productions

Voice-Overs etc.:

Featured talker in;
    "American Talkers: The Art Of The Pitchman"

Point-of-purchase Recordings
    Stores, trade shows, theaters, and carnivals;
            list on request

Talk Show guest on numerous radio talk shows

Specifications:
Age Range	53-62
Height	5' 9.5"
Weight	225 Lbs.
Chest	43.5
Waist	42
Hips	44
Suit	46 Regular
Shirt	16.5-17, 35
Trouser	44 waist, 30 inseam
Shoes	10-10.5
Hair	Lite Brown
Eyes	Brown
Passport	Canada

Ray is legally blind (NYS CBVH# D6527L)

Yenz Von Tilborg

Yenz Von Tilborg

First of all, I am 6.1 tall 175 lb, green eyes and long curly hair, I would not describe my self as wow beautiful, but very different from the normal. I know for sure, people always remember me, even if they only have seen me once, good is some situations, and bad in others (smile).

Well I know for sure, I am good in historical movies and fantasy, my strength in acting is drama, many see me as a bit of Johnny Deep, and I can see my self in same roles he play, and in his kind of movies. I am good in playing strong personalities, I played back in 1978 the Danish poet Hans Cristian Andersen as young, because I have the same profile like him.

As you probably can see in the picture of me, fantasy figure like Dracula would fit perfect to me. As you can see, I never told you my age, and no one really know my age, because I am against to put a number on me, and getting judged by that, so that's why I walk my way through life, not remembering the year I was born.

Educational background.

4 years of acting school in Denmark
4 years school in Hairdressing
2 years school of Film make up
10 years of Classical Ballet school in Denmark

I am born in Denmark, I have lived in countries like, Germany, England, Nederland and now USA.

An innovator in hair concepts and techniques, I have worked internationally, leading the design and creative teams for some of the world's most recognized names. Serving as Lead Artist and Show Coordinator for some of Europe's elite houses of style, I have an unparalleled creativity as well as knowledge of techniques and products. Most recently I served as International Creative Director for Farouk Systems International where my training techniques were the critical element to the continued success of Farouk Systems in the international market.

My formal training lead to my success as a freelance artist, where my talent and vision was repeatedly sought after by some of the most recognized production houses, beauty products and hair care companies throughout the world. More specifically, over the past two decades, my services have been requested by such companies as **Paramount Pictures, Wella Studios** in Copenhagen and Amsterdam, **La Bisothetique** in Denmark and Germany, **TrendyHair** Company, and **Farouk Systems** Europe, and **L'oreal.** Furthermore, I have lent my creativity and talent to both fashion shows and photo shoots for such iconic houses as **Chanel** and **Dior and Karl Lagerfeld.**

My work has been the focus of many articles in international magazines, including **Beautiful You— Made for you, Visagie, Coifure,** and **Top Hair International.** In addition, I have been featured on the cover of **Internetin Business** in an article appropriately title "Business Angels." My life Story and accomplishments have also been published as feature articles in popular industry magazines such as **Les Nouvelles Esthetiques, Paris**.

Currently, I can be seen internationally representing such companies as **John Amico Systems** and **FH1 International,** where I have been working the last 3 years as National Artistic Director and as Director for the Media artist club.

Fluent in six languages, my stage presence transcends international boundaries, making me an invaluable asset to those I represent.

With over 24 years of experience as an educator and as Lead Artist for film makeup and hairstyling, I am highly qualified to represent any company in the United States and abroad. I bring a unique understanding of the beauty industry, from work on film and runway to an ability to share knowledge in highly advanced salon training. I am a valuable team member to any organization. My references are also available upon request.

Yenz von Tilborg

Leona Cyphers

LEONA CYPHERS

AEA, AFTRA, SAG
Brown Hair, Brown Eyes 5'2" – 112 pounds

TELEVISION

SNL – Weekend Update	Bank Manager (Day Player)	NBC
Late Night w/Conan O'Brien	Ms. Gilchrist (Day Player)	NBC
Another World	(Various Under Fives)	NBC
Guiding Light	Betty (Recurring Day Player)	CBS
As The World Turns	(Various Under Fives)	CBS
All My Children	Hospital Administrator (Day Player)	ABC
Loving	Waitress (Recurring Under Fives)	ABC
One Life To Live	(Various Under Fives)	ABC
Tales From the Dark Side	Horrible Witch	Syndicated
Denis Leary's Xmas Special	Nun #1 (Principal)	Comedy Central
Late Show w/David Letterman	Jeff's Mom (Principal)	CBS

OFF BROADWAY

Primal Time	Moonbeam	Theatre Guinevere

OFF-OFF BROADWAY

A Night At The Fights	Disco Darla	(d: Allen Suddeth)
Y.M.C.A.	Acrobat/Athlete	(Rado/Ragni Musical)
Peter Pan	Tiger Lily	Harriman Playhouse
Guys & Dolls	Adelaide	Tompkins Square Playhouse
Company	April	Harriman Playhouse
6 Characters In Search of an Author	Stage Mgr. (Role)	(d: Terry Schreiber)

FILM

The Siege	Paramedic (Day Player)	(d: Ed Zwick)
Women At West Point	Registrar (Day Player)	(Movie of the Week)
Prudential Bache	Account Exec	(Industrial)
Citibank	Jane Davis	(Industrial)
Verizon	Doctor	(Industrial)

COMMERCIALS & PRINT – LIST UPON REQUEST

TRAINING

Wynn Handman, Viveca Lindfors, Rita Gardner, Bill Hickey, Michael Shurtleff, Terry Schreiber, James Litt, Peter Miner

SPECIAL SKILLS

Tennis, Volleyball, Swimming, Bowling, Folk Dancing, Calisthenics, Driver (automatic & stick shift), Golf, Bicycling, Quiltmaker; B.S. in Physical Education. Have valid passport.

Ray DeFeis

Ray DeFeis

SAG / AFTRA

Height: 5'8"
Weight: 140 lbs.
Hair: Brn w/Grey
Eyes: Hazel Grn.

BEST PERFORMANCE BY AN ACTOR for "BLANKOUT" - CHICAGO SHORT FILM FESTIVAL 2006

FILM

BLANKOUT	Edward (Lead)	Cameo Productions, NY
ABSOLUTE	Barry (Lead)	Cinema Verite Productions
PLAYBACK	Jake (Lead)	NYFA, 2007 NY Film Fest.
STRINGER	Elie Semoun Body Dbl.	Klaus Biedermann Paris/NY
NINJA TURTLES 2	Gang Leader	Golden Harvest Productions
JACOBS LADDER	Psycho Patient	IRS (an Adrian Lynne Film)
LITTLE WOMEN	Chingaling	ERRE Productions (Italy)

TELEVISION

CANTERBURY'S LAW	Prisoner #1	FOX – Mike Figgis, Dir.
MAURY POVICH SHOW	Voyeur Uncle	Studios USA Talk Prod.
CONNIE CHUNG SPECIAL	Junkie	CBS (Sunset Park)
SLAVERY AND THE MAKING OF AMERICA	Sentry	PBS National Broadcast

THEATRE

JUNGLELAND	Al Mazucci (Lead)	The Producers Club, NYC
AMBULANCE DANCE	Dr. Goldman (Lead)	Altered Stages, NYC
SOUL SURVIVOR	Brian (Lead)	The Glines, NYC
TYRONE X	Toxic Son	Westbeth Theatre, NYC
NO EXIT	Cradeau (Lead)	Women's Interart , NYC
THE FANTASTICS	Mortimer	Libertyville Playhouse, IL
THE YOUNG BARD	All Characters	National Children's Tour

VIDEO

I WANT TO GET AHEAD (Music Video)	Principle Actor	HBO/WHT/Cinemax

INTERNET

E-Z Smart Blood Glucose Monitor	Doctor (Principle Actor)	Herman Bros. Productions

TRAINING

Acting:	On-Camera Audition, NYC	Alexa Fogel
	Actors Institute, NYC	Dan Fauci / Sally Fisher
	Women's Interart, NYC	Julie Rielly
Improvisational Theatre:	Dudley Riggs, MN	John Remmington
Voice:	Actors Institute, NYC	Ellie Ellsworth
Movement:	Fauntleroy Promotions, NYC	Morse Donaldson

SPECIAL SKILLS

SPORTS

Parachuting, Horseback Riding (Western), Sharpshooter, Track, Baseball, Football,
Soccer, Basketball, Volleyball, Billiards, Bowling, Horseshoes, Rope Climbing

OTHER CAPABILITIES

Commercial Model for Print , Construction Background, Social Dancer, Willing to perform nude

CYCLONE

Jack "Cyclone" Silfen

Hair: Brown
Eyes: Brown
Height: 5'11 1/2"
Weight: 275

INDEPENDENT FILMS:

On the QT	Train Passenger	Platform Productions
Acts of Worship	Bodyguard	Manifesto Films
Particles of Truth	Drunk	Matter Productions
Clearview	Detective	Blue Marble Films

STUDENT FILMS:

Sushi Surprise	Sleazy Camera Guy	Ah-Lien Pictures

TELEVISION:

All My Children	Perp	ABC-TV
Now & Again	Book Burner	Paramount TV
Big Apple	Gambler	Paramount TV
OZ	Third Base Coach	OZ Productions
ESPN's 2 Minute Drill	Contestant Stand-in	ESPN

INDUSTRIALS:

Internet Expo	Santa Claus	Trilogy
Pseudo Movie Opening	Paparazzi	Barry Dean Commun. Corp.
Restaurant History	Burger Guy	The Edge Production Comp.
Chipolte Burrito Lover	Cowboy	Believe Media

PRINT:

Amuzement Japan Magazine	Cover Shoot(Biker)	Yukio Media Comp.
Occupational Stock	Wrestler	Dynamic Graphics Inc.

VOICEOVERS:

NHL Promos	Team Cheers	FOX Sports

MUSIC VIDEOS:

Alicia Keys	Prison Guard	Squeak Pictures Inc./TP
Japanese Karaoke Video	Thug	Underdog Films
Lenny Kravitz	Roadie	Partisan Productions

COMMERCIALS:

Conflicts available upon request

TRAINING:

Kingsborough Community College	Broadcasting Major
LIU (Downtown Brooklyn)	Mass Media Major
Voiceovers Unlimited	Dan Duckworth
Weist-Barron: Technique/Scene Study	David Shuman
Weist-Barron: Advanced Commercial	Batt Johnson and Jerry Coyle
Weist-Barron: Acting for Film & TV	Peter Miner
TVi: Cold Reading Technique	John Mabry
TVi: Commercial Technique	Judy Bowman
TVi: Audition Technique	Dani Super

SPECIAL SKILLS:

Played semi-pro baseball, sports play-by-play, shoot pool, grappling, Kali, Muay-Thai kickboxing, can handle MOST weapons, NYS Security Guard License, NYS CDL Class C Drivers License

Kit Carson McGuire

KIT CARSON MCGUIRE

Height: 5'6"
Weight: 165
Hair: gray/brown
Eyes: blue

FILM

The Rookie	baseball fan	98 MPH Productions/John Lee Hancock
Half Life of a Memory	wizard	jefwuzhere Production/Jef Greilich
The Wendell Baker Story	baptism parishioner	Franchise Pictures/Andrew Wilson
Visions	tourist	24 Hour Film Festival/Damon Chang, Jeffrey Travis
Sin City	lowlife bar patron	Troublemaker Films/Robert Rodriguez
Poodle Dog Lounge	barfly	Blue Tide Films/Daryll Kreitz
Day X	scientist/zombie	Machine City Productions/Jason Bounds
Deadbacks	Mr. Clark	Sabrecat Productions LLC/Aaron Alston
"Z" Zomburbia	zombie grandpa	Dancing Zombies/John McLean
Claire's Triangles	psychologist	Barrett C. Eidson
Demon Board	1st Mate	B-Films Productions/Jeff Cooper
The Hitcher (2006)	motel desk clerk	David Meyers/Director
I'll Come Running	restaurant patron	Spencer Parsons/Director
Grind House: Death Proof	restaurant patron	Quentin Tarantino/Director
Fortune Teller	Dr. McGuire	B-Films Productions/Jeff Cooper
Theft Of The Drag Queen's Wig	Evangelist window washer	Silly Bunny Pictures/Paul Bright

COMMERCIALS

Whole Food Market	fast eating customer	Greg Leonard/Director
PSA for "Hatred"	featured lead	Jayson Oaks/Director

THEATER

The Ugly American	angry villager	Rocky River, Ohio/William Racine-Director

CLASSES

Advanced acting skills	C. K. McFarland & Steve Prince

SKILLS

Radio air personality, musician (12/6 string guitars (60's folk-rock)), computer technician, Professional photographer. Horseback riding.

Shayna
The Juggling Entertaina
& All That Jazz

Shayna
The Juggling Entertaina

FUNCTIONAL SUMMARY

**Shayna Caul, aka Shayna, the Juggling Entertaina,
learned to juggle in her fifties.** She created a dance/juggling
routine to ALL THAT JAZZ while playing with her props and
dancing around the gym. She's performed her signature ALL
THAT JAZZ routine on television, in theatres, for thousands
of jugglers at juggling festivals around the country, for
Connecticut Govenor Jodi Rell, at concerts, weddings, cabarets
and community events. She's given juggling workshops at
corporations and universities. Shayna was a trainer with
Cirque De Soleil's Circus Arts Program. She was a
volunteer HaHa clown at Stamford Hospital and also served on
the HaHa Board of Trustees. She is a retired educator from the
New York City public school system where she worked for 27
years with the roughest and toughest special education
populations in high schools in the South Bronx, Spanish
Harlem and Brooklyn. She edited the nationally acclaimed
magazine, "SPECIAL EDition" and was a staff developer for
the Board of Education and the United Federation of Teachers.
Through a grant, she worked with *The Big Apple Circus
Educational Program.* **Shayna appears in DVDs :
Trailblazers, Women Who Juggle, and The 58th
International Juggling Festival "JAZZ AND
JUGGLING".**

EDUCATION

Brooklyn College 1966-1972
Master of Science, Bachelor of Science, Cum Laude

SUMMARY OF
QUALIFICATIONS AND
AWARDS

- Shayna appears in various **JUGGLER** magazine
  articles, photos and tributes.
- "It's a Tossup"is an extensive two page article about
  Shayna, in **THE ADVOCATE,** 8/2/04.
- Shayna nominated National Teacher of the Year '02.
- NYC's Chancellor visited Shayna's innovative teaching
  program.
- Shayna's featured in "The New York Teacher".

Jade Esteban Estrada

Prince of Pride

JADE ESTEBAN
ESTRADA

Actor/Singer/Dancer/Stand-Up Comic   5'10"

155 lbs

Non-Union

www.GetJaded.com

Film

The Bad Singer	Roman Savage (lead)	Theadora Grey-Dir.
EasyKill	Leo Brody (lead)	Neal Barenblat-Dir.
El Hombre de las Tortugas	Compton	Andrea Zarate-Dir
Ninja Please	Carlos	Joseph Bakhash-Dir.
Quoi? L'Eternite!	Self	French Documentary
Erwachsen Werden	Drag Queen/Stripper	Linda Brieda-Dir. (German)
The Legacy of Walter Frumm	Cal	Jordan Schachter-Dir.
The Perfect Fit	Gay Guy #1	Ron Brown-Dir.
Scent of a Woman	Student	Martin Brest-Dir.

Television

The Graham Norton Effect	S&M Bottom	Comedy Central
Quintessential...New York	Host	Voom HD Network
In the Life TV	Guest Spokesperson	PBS/Andrea Swift-Dir.
The Shield-Episode 213	Musical Artist	FX Network
Into Character	Richie Valens (stand-in)	AMC
In My Lifetime (pilot)	Office Manager	Devin Hampton-Dir.
Jade Esteban Estrada: Live from Heldenplatz	Self	ATV (Austria)
Que Pasa, Hawaii	On-Air host	Oceanic TV
The Jerry Springer Show (2x)	Candy Box	NBC
Best Guest of the Year		
Lydia Mendoza: La Gloria de Tejas	Manuel Mendoza	PBS

Solo Theatre

ICONS Vol. 3	All roles	U.S. Tour
TransWorld!	All roles	U.S. Tour
ICONS Vol. 2	All roles	U.S. Tour
2004 Audience Favorite Award in Solo Performance		
Tortilla Heaven	All roles	U.S. Tour
ICONS Vol. 1	All roles	U.S. Tour
It's Too Late...It's Already in Me	All roles	Jump-Start Theatre-Texas

New York Theatre

Tropical! The Latin Revue	Singer/Dancer #1	Museo del Barrio
Beirut	Blue	Flatiron Theatre
The Boy from Minnesota	Candy Box/Larry	Trocadero Cabaret
One Day Wonder	Tye	Total Theatre Lab
The Plot	Geoffery	Wings Theatre
The Greening of Rosita	Vincent	Nick Corley-Dir.

International

Starlight Express	Flat Top/Caboose	Stella Musicals-Germany
Ocean Dome	Lead Singer	SeaGaia Resorts-Japan
By George, It's Gershwin!	Lead Singer	Allan Blackburn-England
Cirque LeMasque	Lead Dancer/Choreo.	Teresa Careno-Venezuela

Special Skills
Spanish, conversational German, French, Japanese, Choreographer, Playwright, Driver's License, University Lecturer

Awards
2006 Entertainer of the Year, 2005 Performance Artist of the Year, 2004 Audience Favorite in Solo Performance, 2002 Premio Estrella, 2001 Pageantry Magazine Spirit Award

Ron Fagan

Ronald A. Fagan   SAG E

Height 6'1" Weight 210 lbs

Film & Television:

Harold and Kumar 2 Random Passenger (speaking/supporting) HK Prod. Greg Shapiro
Stephen King's The Mist Market Guy Frank Darabont
Fred starring role Fred/Kieth Shively   http://youtube.com/watch?v=thmMcZ-k8BU
IF/First Dawn speaking role TD Productions
Super Villans, Inc. - Television Reporter
FRED starring role "Fred" Keith Shively
Sordid Lives   Insanity Ron   Del Shores

Theatre:

Julius Caesar - Octavius
The Wizard of Oz - Wicked Witch of the West
The Odd Couple - Felix Unger
Twelfth Night - Malvolio
Lear - General Lepidus
Sing on, Sweet Land - Six different roles
The Velveteen Rabbit - Mugsy
Fiddler on the Roof - Nachum the Beggar
Brigadoon - Angus McGuffie
Fiddler on the Roof - The Rabbi
Beckett - Bishop of Oxford, Monk
Androcles and the Lion - Spintho

Special Skills:

30 different impressions, "Rubber Face" , sings beautifully, very comical, European and
regional U.S. dialects, speaks French, excellent at improv and sketch comedy

Jack
Finlay

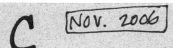

JACK FINLAY

HEIGHT: 5' 11"
WEIGHT: 156 ILB.
HAIR: S&P [DARK BROWN]
EYES: BROWN
D.O.B.: MAY 26, 1959

FILM (PARTIAL LIST)

TERROR INSIDE	FEATURED	GULFCOAST FILM PARTNERS, LLC
TELL HER ABOUT IT	LEAD	F.S.U. FILM SCHOOL
CHASED	LEAD	F.S.U. FILM SCHOOL
BLOOD AND TEARS	SUPPORTING	F.S.U. FILM SCHOOL
SMALL AND FURRY	SUPPORTING	F.S.U. FILM SCHOOL
SPECIAL DELIVERY	SUPPORTING	F.S.U. FILM SCHOOL
MISSING	SUPPORTING	F.S.U. FILM SCHOOL
GEORGE WAS A GOOD MAN	SUPPORTING	F.S.U. FILM SCHOOL
YARD SALE OF DR. DESTRUCTO	FEATURED	F.S.U. FILM SCHOOL
DIRTY POLITICS	FEATURED	F.S.U. FILM SCHOOL
THE DENTIST	FEATURED	F.S.U. FILM SCHOOL

THEATRE (PARTIAL LIST)

THE WIZARD OF OZ	TIN MAN	ANTILLES MIDDLE SCHOOL
ARSENIC & OLD LACE	OFFICER BROPHY	ANTILLES MIDDLE SCHOOL
THE ZOO STORY	PETER	ROOSEVELT RDS. HIGH SCHOOL
OLIVER!	BOW STREET RUNNER	SAMFORD UNIVERSITY
THE MUSIC MAN	CHORUS	ENTERTAINMENT PLUS
OKLAHOMA!	SLIM	ENTERTAINMENT PLUS
THE DRUNKARD	MAGICIAN	TALLAHASSEE LITTLE THEATRE
JOSEPH & THE AMAZING TECH. DREAMCOAT	LEVI	ENTERTAINMENT PLUS
HOW TO SUCCEED IN BUSINESS...	CHORUS	WESLEY PLAYERS
BABY	DOCTOR/PROF. WEISS	OFF STREET PLAYERS
ST. NICHOLAS SPEAKS	SAINT NICK	CHURCH OF THE HOLY SPIRIT
PINNOCHIO	BAD BOY	ATTIC PLAYERS

TRAINING

METHOD ACTING, MAKE-UP	ANTILLES MIDDLE SCHOOL, SAMFORD UNIVERSITY
FILM MAKING	ROOSEVELT ROADS HIGH SCHOOL
VOCAL TRAINING	SAMFORD UNIVERSITY

SPECIAL SKILLS

SINGING (BARITONE), DANCING, PIANO PLAYING, SOUTHERN DRAWL, PUERTO RICAN ACCENT, MULTI-FACIAL EXPRESSIONS, CRYING, LAUGHING, EMOTING, STORYTELLING, PUBLIC SPEAKING, STAND-UP COMEDY, SERIOUS ANGER, SINCERE INSANITY ... I CAN GROW A BEARD QUICKLY....

nikolay

shimunov

height

5'11"

pants

28

inseam

33

suit

36-Atl.

shoe

9

hair

black

eyes

brown

I, AM. Nikolay
SHimunov

My Favorite actors, is.—

1) Steven Seagal
2) Shanh Conner. .007
3) Antonio Baderas,
4) Frank Martin.
5) John Travolta.
6) Charles Bronson.
7) Clinth. Esttwood.—
— etc.

How I came acting and my
bio I give you in person.
Thanks for your interesting.

ORION GALLAGHER

Orion Gallagher

I'm an Actor from Austin, TX 78704. I'm 5'9, 300 lbs with bald hair, Hazel eyes.

PRINT:
Thing's Celtic 2007 Calendar - Mr April - Thing's Celtic

FILM:
The Adventures of Smiley Livingstone - Columbian Druglord - Dir: Tim Hintsala
Deadland Dreaming - crowd scene - Dir. Alan Ray Dream/Walker Pic
Theft - Leatherman #1 - Dir. Paul Bright
Provenance - Shadow dancer - Producers: Mulford/Buesnel
Forgiveness - Audience member - Writer/Director Mariusz Kotowski
Untitled - smoking guy - Director Andrew Bujalski

TELEVISION:
Friday Night Lights - Episode 16: Panther Fan
Friday Night Lights - Episode 17: Bar Patron
Friday Night Lights - Episode 20: Fan

INDUSTRIAL:
Dell Gamers Live Action - Pirate - Southwest Casting

This picture is a tribute to my grandfather, an artist and visionary working at the beginning of the modern era of advertising and graphic design, who was also a bookbinder. In addition to many other clients, he worked for Walt Disney, and he manufactured the Ouija Board from about 1936-1966, although he was not the inventor/owner of the game. In 1966 the Ouija Board set a record for the most games ever sold, a record that has not been broken. The games came from his factory in Philadelphia, Pennsylvania, and were shipped all over the world. It was a big part of pop culture and an important part of my childhood. I guess you can say that the Ouija Board helped me to have a generous imagination, think outside the box, and be aware of my emotions and spirituality.

Being an actress allows me to follow a Bohemian path. I have had the opportunity to work in TV, Film, and commercials on both coasts, although I'm currently working on the east coast. I find it fascinating to see how casting directors cast me in character and type, and I find it just as challenging convincing them that I can be someone they hadn't imagined. My home base is Pennsylvania, where my stage name Renee "Philly" Fishman was born.

My favorite jobs are when I feel that I am really adding something valuable to a project, which I get to do more often than you would think. As a Registered Nurse, I lend reality to a medical scene. And I've been everything from a southern belle to a cafeteria worker, a nun to a Hasidic Jew, and a prisoner to a court stenographer.

The passion of taking a character and making it your own, different from anything that's been done before, has filled 7 closets of my home with period clothing from 1890 to the present day, costumes, accessories and props. I always say, "Give me an hour, and I'll create anything you want."

My industry jobs, experiences, and adventures have taken my love for storytelling to a whole new place, as I have always enjoyed putting smiles on people's faces.

I like to remember the words of my grandfather -- "Whatever you do, be sure to give back to the community what the community gives to you." That's a principle I try to follow.

Renee "Philly" Fishman

SAG/AFTRA

Robert Strong

Robert Strong

Age: 35
Height: 5'10"
Weight: 185

Hair: Brown
Eyes: Brown

Magician, Juggler, & Comedian (1985- Present)
The Kennedy Center, DC
The Las Vegas Convention Center, NV
The Lyric Opera House, MD
The Magic Castle, CA
The White House, DC
Disney Cruise Lines, FL
Jacob Javitz Convention Center, NY

Training
20 Years of Performing Experience
Mid-Atlantic Movement Theater Festival
45^E Festival International De Jonglerie
70th Annual International Brotherhood of Magicians Convention
Two year Graduate of Louis Tannen's Magic School
Ringling Brothers and Barnum Bailey Circus Clown Workshops
Graduate of Towson State University's College of Fine Arts and Mass Communications
MotionFest Instructor
San Francisco Circus Center Instructor

Special Skills
Fire Eating	Ballroom Dancing	Slapstick/Physical Comedy
Stilt Walking	Escape Artist	Pick-Pocket
Unicycling	Chainsaw Juggling	Public Speaking

Theatre
Fire Schtick	Master of Ceremonies
Vaudeville	The Great Strongdini
1st-5th Continental Congress of Jugglers	Master of Ceremonies
Circus Beyond	Ringmaster
Hagen, Germany Juggling Festival	Compere

Television
"Fox 45 Clubhouse"	Guest Magician
"Home Team Sports"	10' Tall Umpire
"ABC News"	Featured Entertainer
"NBC News"	Featured Entertainer
"CBS This Morning"	Featured Street Performer
"It's Kindertime"	Guest Juggler

Commercial
Harrahs	Circus Clown
Wampler Longacre	Stale Turkey on the Late Bus
Magic Me	Host

Industrial
Super Fresh	Master Chef

Print
Baltimore Magazine	Model
The Washington Post	Feature Article
Jugglers World	Fire Juggler at the White House

Amy Lyndon

AMY LYNDON
SAG/AFTRA

FILM (*Extremely Partial List*)

B.T.K.	Lead	Lions Gate/Michael Feifer
Bram Stokers Dracula's Guest	Lead	Lions Gate/Michael Feifer
The House That Jack Built (w/Joe Mantegna)	Supporting	Dir: Bruce Reisman
The Poughkeepsie Tapes	Supporting	MGM/John Dowdle
Chicago Massacre: Richard Speck	Supporting	Lions Gate/Michael Feifer
Ed Gein - The Butcher of Plainfield	Supporting	Lions Gate/Michael Feifer
Trinity: Gehenna	Lead	Dir: Dan Jacobson
Are You Scared	Supporting	Lions Gate/Andy Hurst
Big City Blues	Supporting	Showtime/Clive Fleury
Forever In Love	Supporting	Showtime/Rob Spera
An Angel Named Billy	Lead	Dir: Greg Osborne
Cursed Part 3	Starring	Dir: Rae Dawn Chong
Some Enchanted Evening	Lead	Dir: Reuban Simon
Horror High	Lead	Dir: Shawn Papazian
Living The Dream	Supporting	Dir: Christian Schoyen
Apocalypse Oz	Supporting	Dir: Ewan Telford
Thin Ice (Best Actress Nominee)	Starring	Dir: Rick Garside
The Epiphany	Starring	Dir: Beverly Samuell
Waiting Game	Lead	Dir: Christopher Ver Wiel
Boy In The Box	Lead	Dir: Screaming Mad George
Divorce: The Musical	Lead	Dir: Steven Dworman
Slaves Of Hollywood	Lead	Dirs: T. Keefe/M. Wechsler
Pacino Is Missing	Lead	Dir: Eric Galler
Glitch!	Lead	Dir: Nico Mastorakis
A Night In Heaven	Supporting	Warner Brothers/John Avildsen

TELEVISION (*Partial List*)

Ugly Betty	Guest Star	ABC/Lev L. Spiro
Entourage	Guest Star	HBO/Julian Farino
Gene Simmons Family Jewels	Special Guest Star	A & E/Various
Valley of the Cougars	Special Guest Star	PILOT/Tim Schaaf
NYPD Blue	Guest Star	ABC/Mark Tinker
The Young And The Restless	Recurring Lead	CBS/Various
The Bold And The Beautiful	Recurring Lead	CBS/Deveney Kelly
General Hospital	Recurring	ABC/Marlena Laird
JAG	Guest Star	CBS/Terrence O'Hara
Providence	Guest Star	NBC/Mike Fresco
Roswell	Guest Star	WB/David Semel
18 Wheels Of Justice	Guest Star	TNN/Rob Hedden
Married… with Children	Guest Star	FOX/Amanda Bearse
Galaxy Beat	Recurring/PILOT	CBS/Les Landau
On The Lot	Series Regular	PILOT/Nick Siconolfi
Da Mob	Series Regular	FOX FAMILY PILOT
Freddy's Nightmare (**Recurring**)	Guest Lead	FOX/Gil Adler
Trial By Jury	Guest Lead	NBC/Marty Pasetta, Jr.
Almost Grown	Guest Star	CBS/Joan Tewksbury

Extensive Theatre List Available Upon Request

TRAINING/SPECIAL SKILLS

Acting:	Stella Adler, Harry Mastrogeorge, Al Ruscio, Glen Casale, Nick Siconolfi, Arthur Storch (NYC)
Formal:	Neighborhood Playhouse (NYC), Syracuse University (BFA), London Academy Of Performing Arts
Comedy:	The Groundlings, Int'l Blend Troupe (w/Rick Overton), The Comedy Store, CBS on the Lot (Paul Ryan)
Dialects:	Eastern European, Cockney, Southern, British, All New York, Hungarian
Additional:	Booking Coach/Acting Teacher (16 years), Voice-Over Artist, Filmmaker, Art Photographer, Physical Comedy
Awards:	**Marquee Comedy Award WINNER** - The Tiffany, Crown Award Nominee - **Best Dramatic Actress** "Thin Ice"

JOHN HENRY SCOTT

JOHN HENRY SCOTT

HEIGHT:6'3" - WEIGHT 196
HAIR:BROWN -EYES:HAZEL
S.A.G
AGE RANGE: late 40's - 60's

TV AND FILM:(all are S.A.G.)REEL ON REQUEST
"THE BIG EASY" -----------JULES------------PRINCIPAL
"GOING TO CALIFORNIA------BO(TRUCKER)-------PRINCIPAe
"MATLOCK-----------------MAINTENANCE MAN----PRINCIPAL
"HOUSE OF SECRETS-------NESTOR-------SUPPORTING ROLE
"ADVENTURES OF HUCK FINN-ABE TURNER--SUPPORTING ROLE
"A DIFFERENT KIND OF CHRISTMAS"-GUARD------PRINCIPAL
"AMERICAN GOTHIC"--------ABUSIVE DAD-------PRINCIPAL
"THE ROSE GARDEN"-------SPOTTER-----------PRINCIPAL
"UNSOLVED MYSTERIES"----A.J.BREAUX---LEAD/TITLE ROLE
"ROAD TO WELLEVILLE"----ATTENDANT----------PRINCIPAL
"DELTA HEAT"-----------JULIOUS RABEAUX-----PRINCIPAL
"FACE ON THE MILK CARTON"---TV REPORTER----PRINCIPAL
"ONE CHRISTMAS---------CARD PLAYER---------PRINCIPAL
"FALLTIME"-------------FARMER--------------PRINCIPAL

STAGE:(just a sampling
HARVEY--ELWOOD P.DOWD---BAYOU DINNER THEATER(N.O.,LA
OUR TOWN---EDITOR WEBB--KENNER REPERTORY THEATER(KENNER,LA.)
NORMAN IS THAT YOU--BEN CHAMBERS--ROSE DINNER THEATER(ALGIERS,LA.)
THE RAINMAKER-----NOAH CURRY---------LEPETITE THEATER(NEW ORLEANS)
ARSENIC AND OLD LACE----JONATHON----STARLIGHT DINNER THEATER(N.O.)
BUS STOP--------VIRGIL BLESSING---ROSE DINNER THEATER(ALGIERS,LA.)
BABES IN TOYLAND------UNCLE BARNABY--KENNER REPERTORY THEATER(LA.)
MUSIC MAN---------CHARLIE COWELL-----KENNER REPERTORY THEATER(LA.)
SCROOGE---------- MARLEY--MINNICAPELLI DINNER THEATER(SLIDELL,LA.)
MASKED MAYHEM(I WROTE IT)GREAT SCOTT-THALIAN HALL-(WILMINGTON.N.C)
-----------------------ETC ETC ETC-------------------------
TRAINING:
SYLVANA GILLARDO---THE ACTING CLASS-----LOS ANGELES

UNIVERSITY OF N.Q.--ADVANCED ACTING TECHNIQUE---N.O.,LA.
THE ACTORS STABLE------THE METHOD---N.0.,LA.
LOTS OF WEEKEND SEMINARS
---------------------ETC.ETC. ETC-------------------SPECIAL SKILLS:
MAGICIAN,MUSICIAN(BASS),STILT WALKER,BALLOON ARTIST,SIDESHOW
PERFORMER,RADIO DJ,CLOWN,HAVE PILOTS LICENSE,SAIL SMALL BOATS,RIDE
MOTORCYCLES,STATIC MIME,CAJUN COMEDY

05   JEFF ZAWADA

JEFFERY ZAWADA

Seeking Agent

Height: 5'9"   **Hair:** Brown
Weight: 170   **Eyes:** Blue
B-Day: 8/26/78

FILM & TELEVISION

Division	Extra LifeTimeProductions
Alias	Extra Disney Productions
Fast Lane	Extra Fox Productions

TRAINING & EDUCATION

Cold Reading	Stephen Snyder	Chicago Studio, Illinois
TV I, II, III	John Robert Powers	Oxnard Office, California

PRINT ADVERTISEMENT
Miller Lite

SPECIAL SKILLS

Light Stunts: staged combat / weaponry / down-hill skiing / snowmobiling / precision driving / stock cars / motorcycles / all other all-terrain vehicles / heavy equipment operator

Physically fit. Recent 2D~ place finish in a Michigan Upper Peninsula Arm Wrestling Competition. Natural Dancer: HipHop, Rap, Country Western music, and can sing as well. Selfdescribed All-American Midwestern Cowboy.

Follows directions; positive attitude; quick-study; works without hidden agenda; strives to learn, self-starter; treats people with respect and dignity; willing to go to any extent to fulfill any job requirements.

So how's everyone doing My names Jeffrey Zawada /An Actor with endless heart. So how long have I heen studying my craft along time Its been an uphill climb the whole way, do I regret the heartache that comes with it, not at all. It seems like yesterday in High school I was the groom for that mock wedding when I originally got the bug. But since then it took yrs before I caught my break for Miller Lite, What a mile stone though. If there's any thing that prepared me for this, I'd say it was a mixture of persistence an patients, along with drive an a whole lot of Heart. I'm a very driven individual, always have been always will be, an as far as one word of advice for up an coming talent, always preparing yoursel for your next job! Weather Its in the Industry or busin tables. My influences consist of Vetran's such as Bruce Willis, Robert Deniro, James Dean, Chevy Chase, just to name a few. My favorite movies are endless, but again a couple that come to mind would be Goodwill Hunting, Walking Tall, Pearl Harbor, a Man Apart! Dukes of Hazzard, Serendipity, depending on my mood I guess. So I just want too thank those who came before me an those who'll rise above me, an keep me striving for perfection, it's been a heck a ride Thanks again. Sincerely, **Jeffrejames**

RACHEL WITZ

Height: 5'6"
Eyes: Grey
Hair: Red

FILM

"Christmas In New York"	Snake Woman	Dir. Neri Parenti
"Misunderstood"	Rita (Gay Racist)	Dir. Marcus Ziegler
"If Only He'd Call"	Emma (Bitchy best friend)	Dir. Sandra Beltrao
"The Dreamcatcher"	Kim Russell (Defense Attorney)	K.T. Productions
"Doctor's Orders"	Laura (Tourette Syndrome)	K.T. Productions

TELEVISION

Rachael Ray Show	Self/Horror Actor	New York

THEATER

"Bayside 2 – Electric Screechio"	Screech !	Incredio Productions
"Bayside the Un-Musical"	Screech (Saved by the Bell)	Incredio Productions
"Inconvenience of Death"	Marlene (Needy Italian) T.S.I.	

STAND-UP

Caroline's On Broadway	New York City	New York
Stand-up NY	New York City	New York
NY Comedy Club	New York City	New York
Citigroup Inc.	New York City	New York

SPECIAL SKILLS

Comedian, Writer, Imitations, Voices, Development of unique Characters, Accents: British, Southern, French, Russian, German, Mid-West, Singer, Songwriter, Freestyle Dance, Lip Sync, Makeup Artist, Athletic, New York State Drivers License

TRAINING

School for Film and Television
Second City (New York)
The Barrow Group
HB Studio
Stand-up NY
TVI Studios
Manhattan School of Comedy

EDUCATION

Fashion Institute of Technology (F.I.T.), New York
Associate in Applied Science in Interior Design

ON THE SIDE

Freelance Makeup Artist

Jason Collins

JASON COLLINS

Height: 5'8"   Hair Color: Brown
Weight: 160   Eye Color: Brown

TELEVISION

CAMELBACK NEWS	On-Camera Talent	Closed Circuit TV

INDUSTRIAL

BEST BUY	Principal	Training Video

PROMOTIONAL

RAINFOREST CAFÉ	Spokesperson	Denver, CO
RADIO	Promote Night Clubs & Stations throughout Denver	Denver, CO

VOICEOVER

GRIFFIN PRODUCTIONS	Movie Trailer	Home Video
HAUNTED CORN FIELD	Radio Commercial	Denver, CO

TRAINING

JULIE IRELAND	Improvisational Comedy Class.	Denver, CO
ELIZABETH SAVAGE TALENT	Post Secondary Certified	
	Commercial Acting Class.	Phoenix, AZ
ELIZABETH SAVAGE TALENT	Scene Study Class.	Phoenix, AZ
BROADCAST SCHOOL	Certificate-Television/Radio	Denver, *CO*
RADIO	103.5 THE FOX Lewis & Floorwax Assistant Producer	Denver, CO

SPECIAL SKILLS

Voice-overs – Have very deep speaking voice
Singing(Influence, Love shack, Spin me round like a record 'sounding')
Dancing
Play the Trumpet
Horseback Riding
Motorcycle Riding

SPORTS/HOBBIES

Remote Controlled Aircraft ~ Inline-Skating ~ Basketball ~ Football ~ Street Hockey ~
Jet Skiing ~ Weight Training ~ Hiking ~ Climbing ~ Paintball

MARK WENZEL

MARK WENZEL

SAG - AFTRA
HEIGHT - 6'
WEIGHT - 150
HAIR - BROWN
EYES - BROWN

FILMS

BORN IN EAST L.A.	FEATURED BIT	WARNER BROTHERS
SAY YES	FEATURED BIT	FAUNT LEROY PRODUCTIONS
RETURN OF THE KILLER TOMATOES	FEATURED BIT	FOUR SQUARE PRODUCTIONS

TELEVISION

CYCLING THROUGH CHINA	SMITH/HEMION PRODUCTIONS
PM MAGAZINE	GROUP W PRODUCTIONS
THE FORD 75TH ANNIVERSARY SHOW	BOB BANNER PRODUCTIONS
PERRY COMO'S EASTER BY THE SEA	BOB BANNER PRODUCTIONS
CIRCUS OF THE STARS	BOB STIVERS PRODUCTIONS

STAGE

FANTASTIKS	MUTE/MORTIMOR	WESTGATE DINNER THEATRE
SPOKESONG	TRICK CYCLIST	MARQUIS PUBLIC THEATRE
ANDROCLES & THE LION	ANDROCLES	SAN DIEGO REPERTORY THEATRE
KING RICHARD II	LORD WILLOUGHBY	OLD GLOBE THEATRE
CACTUS FLOWER	IGOR	HAMPTON PLAYHOUSE
FORTUNE & MEN'S EYES	MONA	HAMPTON, N.H.

COMMERCIALS

LIST AVAILABLE UPON REQUEST

INDUSTRIAL FILMS

S.D. CON. & VIS. BUREAU	FISHER STEREO	SEA WORLD
U.S. NAVY	S.D. BLOOD BANK	S.D. BOARD OF EDUCATION
HOME FEDERAL S&L	TAMARCK PROPERTIES	OAK INDUSTRIES

VARIETY

OFFICIAL MIME-EXPO '84 & '86-WORLD'S FAIRS
LOS ANGELES COUNTY FAIR-OFFICIAL MIME SINCE 1979-WORLD'S LARGEST COUNTY FAIR
SEA WORLD-RESIDENT MIME-8 YEARS-ENTERTAINING OVER ONE MILLION PEOPLE ANNUALLY
COMEDY STORE, IMPROV, FAIRS, CRUISE SHIPS, SCHOOLS, UNIVERSITIES AND MAGAZINE COVERS

ABILITIES

UNICYCLIST   JUGGLER   FENCER   SCUBA DIVER   MIME

TRAINING

BACHELOR OF ARTS: UNITED STATES INTERNATIONAL UNIVERSITY,
SAN DIEGO AND LONDON CAMPUSES

COMMERCIAL ACTING:	BERNYCE CRONIN
STAGE:	WALTER COY, CURT CONWAY
DIRECTION:	ASSAD KELADA
DICTION:	DENNIS TURNER
VOICE OVER:	SOUND TRAX

Susyn Timko

SUSYN TIMKO
SAG/AFTRA

Film
Absentee	Starring	Dir. Bob Moore
Strategies	Starring	Dir. Don Peterson
Commitment	Starring	Dir. Don Peterson
Cathy	Lead	Dir. Sam Chow

Television
I'm Beautiful	Principle	Dir. Margaret Cho
Mpower TV	Special Guest	www.mpowertv.com

Theater
New York Theatre
Steel Magnolias	Shelby	New York Performance Works
Street Car Named Desire	Stella	New York Performance Works
Who's Afraid of Virginia Wolf	Honey	The Producer's Club
The Star Spangled Girl	Sophie	The Producer's Club
A Texas Trilogy	LuAnn Hampton	New York Performance Works
Life and Limb	Effie	The Producer's Club
Please Don Not Disturb	Nina	Creative Place Theatre
The Role Of Delia	Emma	Dir. Beth Dalton

Comedy
The Comedy Store, Comedy Underground, Stand-Up New York, New York Comedy Club, Don't Tell Mama, Gotham Comedy Club, Ye Olde Triple Inn

Training
Acting	The Lyndon Technique/Amy Lyndon
Acting	Margie Habor
Acting	William Esper 2 year program/NYC
Acting	Irma Sandry/Lee Strasberg Inst./NYC
Acting	Lynette Sheldon/NYC
Commercial	Joan See/AIA The Three Of Us
Comedy/Improv	The Groundlings
Stand-Up	Greg Dean
Stand-Up	Tim Davis

Other Experience
Singing: Coloratura Soprano (Pop/R&B/Country/Musical Theatre)
Musical Instruments: Piano, Vibra-Slap
Performance: Improvisation, Short Form, Sketch Comedy, Multiple Character's, Vocal Characterizations, and Jump Rope
Dance: Disco, Modern, Waltz, Polka, and Improvisational
Dialects: Brooklyn, Southern
Sports: Aerobics, Badminton, Baton Twirling, Bowling, Cheer Leading, Frisbee, Ice Skate, Jogging, Roller Skate, Running, Soccer, Softball, Volley ball, Bicycling, Hiking, Tennis, Yoga, Golf
Additional skills: Songwriter, Children's Party Performer, Magic Tricks, Face Painting, Balloon Animals

Mr. Greeber

Dale Greeber

Actor
Moddel

STAGES:

Here We Are Again Going	Jenz	Reykjavik Theatre
Don't Do That So Hard	Chorus	Malmo Public House

FILMS:

Trorr Dem Lauser Fiske Mo (Song of the Fish-God)	Walter
Nixon: Dem Beserker	Kissinger
Dem Monica Lewinsky Stuury	Dad
Simm, Simm, Mongen Inten Hesten (Frisk, Frisk, Gentle Pony)	Pony's friend

INDUSTRIEL FILMS:

Pork: Know the Dangers	Angry Farmer
Spoorn Men im Denken Jemm (Tools Are Our Friends)	Narrator

COMERCIALS: No comercials.

VOICES OVER: He do the **voices over.**

HE can speak Swedish and German and some French. Can **Khazakh dialects** and also Russian Czech French German Irish Hindi Dutch and Swedish ones.

SKILS:
Curling, fishing, spearing, wisk broom, bucket, good of looks; takes many women quickly; spoor find; hammer, tools, gender sensitivity,negotiation.

HOBIES:
HE does Krimble dances; Skiing, Curling, Swimming; Traditional Norse Mud-Castling; To see the Eclipse; Fish-calls; Allergic to shellfish

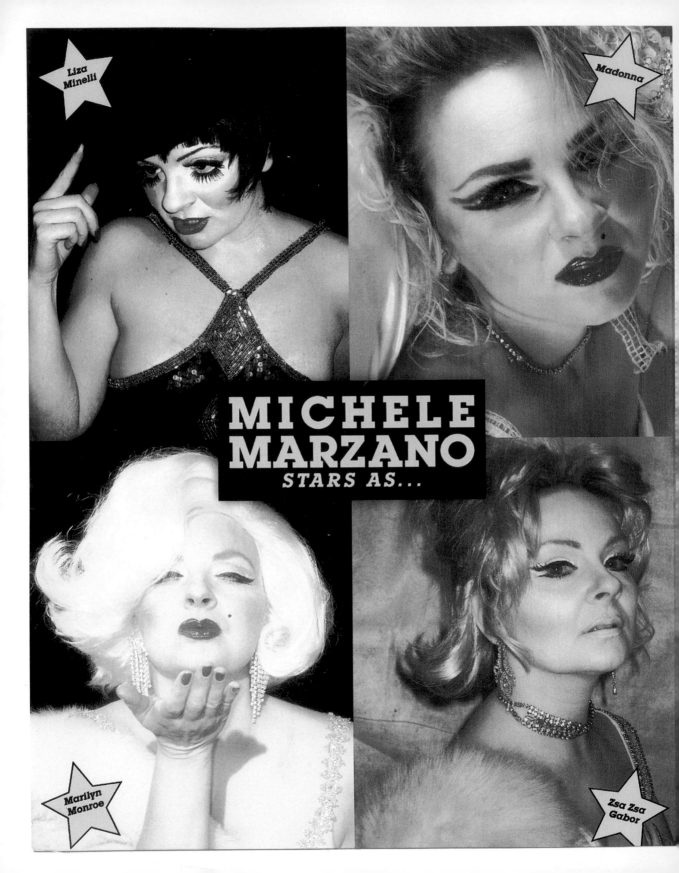

Liza Minelli

Madonna

MICHELE
MARZANO
STARS AS...

Marilyn Monroe

Zsa Zsa Gabor

MICHELE MARZANO

Hair: Blonde
Eyes: Blue/Green

THEATER
An Awesome 80's Prom Night	Madonna (Principal)	Off-Broadway
		Ken Davenport

VIDEO
Bon Jovi	B.Q.F.M. (Principal)	TBJ Productions

TELEVISION
Forensic Files	Debbie Timlock (Principal)	Court TV
The Maury Show	Lead (Re-Enactment)	NBC
Ricki Lake Show	Madonna (Principal)	UPN

FILM
The Bar	Janis Joplin (Principal)	Richard Stern

PRINT
Iodonna	Elizabeth Taylor Look-A-Like	Milan, Italy

SINGING
Exit 9 "Tonight"	Background Vocals	7th Sign Records
Lead Vocals	Various Cover Bands	Standards/Pop/Rock

LIVE PERFORMANCES
Japan Spring 2007	Madonna Impersonation	Tour
31 Days of Oscar	Elizabeth Taylor Look-A-Like	Turner Classic Movies

TALENTS/EXPERIENCE
Various Celebrity Impersonations: Credits Upon Request
Madonna, Marilyn Monroe, Cyndi Lauper, Liza Minelli, Janis Joplin, Stevie Nicks, Carol Channing, Mae West
Model: Print, Stock, Hand, Runway, Tearoom, Promotional

AWARDS
Miss America Scholarship

EDUCATION/TRAINING
B.A. University of Portland
Acting: Stephen Waldrup
Singing: Lee Knight
Modeling: D'Rene'

SKILLS
Extensive wig and costume wardrobe, fortune telling: palm and tarot, speak German well, Lead Singer/
Songwriter, some acoustic Guitar, Makeup Artist

KEVIN COYLE

Kevin Coyle

SAG-AFTRA

Height 6'0"
Eyes: Blue
Weight 180
 Hair: Brown

FILM:

Summer of Sam	Protester	Spike Lee Productions
Godzilla	Secret Service Agent	Big Fin Productions
The Peacemaker	Pedestrian	Dream Works Productions
Deep Impact	Tourist	Dream Works Productions
Celebrity	Theatre Goer	Woody Allen Productions

TELEVISION:

Dave Chapelle Show	Blind Man {Principal Part}	HBO
Saturday Night Live	Contestant	NBC
New York Undercover	Basketball Coach	FOX 5

COMMERCIALS::
Furnished Upon Request

TRAINING::

American Academy	
Weist-Barron	Commercial Course
Seton Hall University	Acting I

SPECIAL SKILLS:

Licensed Driver, Baseball, Basketball, Singing, Fitness

Johnnie Rodriguez

JOHNNIE RODRIGUEZ

Character Actor adept at Physical Comedy and Drama
Height.............5'8
Weight.............160
Eyes..................Brown
Hair....................Salt/Pepper (more salt)

THEATRE
"Looking for Mrs. Santa Claus" numerous roles, Practical Paradox
"Angels" Neal, New Wine Skins Prods.
"In the Summer When it's Hot and Sticky" Hector, Theatre Rhinoceros
"Androcles and the Lion" Androcles, Diablo Performing Arts
"Metamorphis-Us" Improvisational Group, Diablo Valley College
"The Diary of Adam and Eve" Adam, Concord City Chamber of Arts

TELEVISION
"America's Most Wanted" lead, Benson Cruz episode
"Unsolved Mysteries" Felon, Alcatraz episode
"Midnight Caller" Receptionist, Tangled Web episode
"Jesse Hawkes" Drunk, Glass Pipe episode
"I, Detective" Det. Greg Smith, Speeding into Danger episode

FILM
"bUs.tRip"....(In Production)...........Bob
"Amaru"...(In Production)..Pedro Urdemalas
"Someday School"........Grandpa (lead)
"Blood Loss"(the short).........Burton
"Blood Loss"(the feature) (View trailer at www.Lagoonside.com). ..Ulee
"Food Chain"...............Mr. Jerry
"Generating Delusion"....Homeless/Wino
"Top Dog"......... Homeless/Wino
"Bunya"....... Rosa de la Rosa (transsexual)
"The Bench"........Theif
"Desperately Ever After".... Henry Montenegro
"The Imposter"........................ Rafa
"Spontaneous Combustion"........ Interviewee
"The Condemned"......Murderer (lead)
(View The Condemned at www.deepcuts.net)
"The Surrogate"...............lead
"Alice in Storageland"....Miguel (Post Production)
"The Adventures of Sadie"..Animal Rights Activist (Post Production)

COMMERCIAL
•Coors Extra Gold
•Chevron
"Child Neglect" Public Service Announcement
"Domestic Abuse" Public Service Announcement

CD ROM   "The Dark Crystal" Minion

MUSIC VIDEO   "I AM CRUSHED"(by The Vandals).....Lead

INDUSTRIALS
•Sun Microsystem
•Go Corporation
•Kaiser Permanente
•Pacific Bell Telephone

VOICE OVER
"Farming the Seas"...........PBS Documentary
"Los! Big! Names!"............Marga Gomez Show

SPECIAL SKILLS
Juggling-Dancing-Improv-Mime-Bartending-Drawing

STEVE FALK

Steven H. Falk

Eyes: Hazel Hair: Lt. Brown
Height: 6' Weight 175lbs.

Television

Face of America Changing	Audience Member	Parisean Edward
Law & Order	Police Protest	NBC Universal TV
Law & Order	Union Member	NBC Universal TV
Car Less	Bridge Walker	American Gold Pro.
New York Love Story	NY Yankee Baseball Fan	Alternate Current, Inc.

Industrial or Music Video

Faze	Production Crew	Classic Concept
First Alert	Burglar	Aurora 4 Video
Little Wonder	Subway Rider	David Bowie
Destination Anywhere	Club Patron	Bon Jovi

Print or TV Ads

US Air	Traveling Businessman	Coppers Films
Duralube	Car Owner	Future Thunder

Movie

Longtime Companion	Homeless	Companion Pro, Inc.
The Cornfields	Detective Simpson	Duggan Studios
First We Take Manhattan	Hotel Patron	Friend Cheer Pro.
American Shavein	Audience Member	Seasonal Film Corp.
Pushing Hand	Restaurant Patron	Central Motion Picture
Blind Vision	Condo Owner	2 Scorpion Film Pro.
What the Moon Saw	Villager	Sistrum Production Ltd.
All I Know	Hippy	All I Know Productions
Fools Paradise	Traveling Businessman	Good Machine Baby, Inc.
	Airline Ticket Sales	
Practice to Deceive	Track and Field Runner	Bergmann Pro.
Walls and Bridge	Patron of the Arts	Colg Grey Pro.
Clean Sharn	Construction Worker	Kerrigan Pro
A Bronx Tale	Horse Gambler	BT Productions
Die Hard w/Vengeance	Driver-Stockbroker	20th Century Fox
Suits	Businessman	Tinafly Films
Childhoods End	Basketball Referee	Open City
The Money Shot	Partygoer	Money Shot
Crazy	Party-Theatergoer	GM Inc.
Someday Somewhere	Costumes	Kyoda TV
Outsider	Ballroom Dancer	GoatLord
Picture This	Waiter	Albright
The Dance Movie	Audience Member	Columbia Pictures
*Dead Dog	Assistant DA	Dead Dog
Table One	Club Patron	Table One
Chain of Chace	Catholic Priest	Mirror Movies
	Witness Execution	
Tracker	Medic	Two Day Pro.
Brothers Gotta Work It Out	Doctor	NYCH Authority
		- VSE Entertainment
*Steve's Place	Catholic Priest	Trevor Moore Pro.
*Iron Horse	Homeless Man	41/2 Finger Pro.
*Should Heaven Fall	Irish Gangster	Jonathan Basli Pro.
*Some Kind of Awful	Good Ol'boy	Cordell – Pfriender Pro.
*Last Rites	Diner Manager	Insame-o-rama Pro.

VOICE
Different regions of American, English and Irish

SKILLS
NYS Driver's License, Bartender, Football, Baseball, Softball, Basketball & Bicycling

I have costumes or wardrobe for
New York City Policeman & Supervisor Uniform, Tuxedo, Doctor, Cowboy, Etc.

*Where I had speaking parts.

I am sending my resume and picture to you for your upcoming project or production.

145

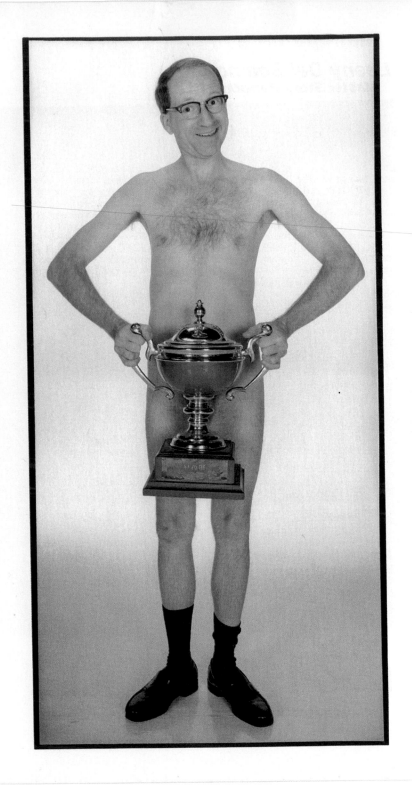

D A V I D

P I R E S

DAVID PIRES
SAG/AFTRA/AEA

Hair: **Light Brown**
Eyes: **Blue**
Height: **5'6"**
Weight: **120lbs**

FILM:

Stamped!	Starring	Frontier Films (Bryce Hatch)
The Moment After 2: Sleepers Awake	Starring	Signal Hill Pictures (Wes Llewellyn)
Fast Track	Supporting	Structure Film Works (Kantz)
Holy Man Undercover	Supporting	Underdog Prods. (David .R. White)
Expired	Supporting	Expired Prods. (Cecilia Miniucchi)
The Last Stand	Supporting	Up To Parr Prods. (Russ Parr)
Durango Kids	Supporting	Good Friends Prods. (Ashton Root)
The Ghost of Spoon River	Supporting	Malibu Prod. (Scott Meehan)
Mr. Saturday Night	Supporting	Castle Rock (Billy Crystal)
Masters Of Menace	Supporting	CineTel Films (Tino Insana)
Zoo Radio	Starring	Wells Entertainment (Jay Roach)

TELEVISION:

Tim and Eric Awesome Show, Great Job!	Recurring	Cartoon Network (Tim & Eric)
The Revengers	Host	VH1 (Jeff Wykoff)
Inside Roller Derby	Reporter	GRDA (Alex Jurrow)
That's Funny	Recurring	Syndicated (David Wechter)
Tom Goes To The Mayor (Cartoon)	Recurring	Cartoon Network (D.J. Paul)
Reasonable Doubt	Supporting	Discovery Channel (Kris Chan)
Power Rangers:Time Force	Guest Star	Saban Ent. (Kaizo Hayashi)
The Best Damn Sports Show Period	Recurring	FOX Sports West (Eric Shanks)
Kenan & Kel	Principal	Nickelodeon (Howard Storm)
The Tonight Show With Jay Leno	9 Sketches	NBC (Various Directors)
Married…With Children	Co-Star	FOX (Sam W. Orender)
Cybill	Supporting	CBS (Andrew D Weyman)
New York Daze	Guest Star	FOX (Steve Zuckerman)
Port Charles	Recurring	ABC (Anthony Morina)
Show Me The Funny	Recurring	Fox Family (David Wechter)
E! True Hollywood Story	Principal	E! (Brent Zacky)
Totally Animals .	Supporting	CBS (Sandi Fullerton)
Slanted Lens	Principal	German TV (Jay P. Morgan)
Crazy Planet	Principal	French TV (Chantal Valois)
The Big Deal	Supporting	Fox (Sandi Fullerton)
Storm The Castle	Supporting	CBS (Steve Santos)
General Hospital	Recurring	ABC (Various Directors)
Santa Barbara	Supporting	NBC (Peter Brinckerhoff)
America's Funniest People	Recurring	ABC (David Wechter)

THEATRE:

Another Evening Without Millard Fillmore	Improv	West End Playhouse (Dennis Dale)
Spoon River Anthology	Ensemble Player	Toluca Lake Players (Doreen Davis)
Career	Jack Goldman	So. City Theatre Co. (Gregory Bach)
A Reverie With Edgar Lee Masters	John Wasson	Illinois Arts Council (David Bishop)
The Lion In Winter	King Phillip	Fulton County Playhouse (Carol Davis)
The Last Of Mrs. Lincoln	Lewis Baker	Fulton County Playhouse (Larry Eskridge)
South Pacific	Bob McCaffrey	Fulton County Playhouse (David Bishop)

(COMPLETE LIST UPON REQUEST)

TRAINING:

Illinois Wesleyan University	Dr. John Ficca	B.F.A. in Theatre Performance
Upfront Comedy	Jane Morris	Improvisation
Weist-Barron-Hill, Los Angeles		
M.G. Kelly's Voice Over Workshop		
Greg Dean's Stand-Up Comedy Workshop		
Gascon Institutes' Academy of Theatrical Combat		

SPECIAL SKILLS AND ABILITIES:

Fencing, Stage Combat, Teacher, Photographer, Emcee, Comedy, Playing Santa Claus,
Tour Guide at Universal Studios, This and That, Nerd Stripper, Ordained Minister

W. A. Walters

AEA SAG AFTRA

W.A.WALTERS
AEA/SAG/AFTRA

Height -- 5'10" Eyes --Blue
Weight -- 150 Hair -- Blond (Long)
Voice – Baritone

TELEVISION (PRINCIPAL/DAY PLAYER/U5)
ED - *Eli's Disciple #1* - Viacom/NBC (Tom Cavanagh)
SUPERMARKET SWEEP - *Puppeteer (Holiday special)* - Talent Associates (David Susskind)
MERV GRIFFIN SHOW - *Specialty Act (Puppeteer)* - Westinghouse/Metromedia

FILM (BACKGROUND)
TALK TO ME (Kasi Lemmon), ENCHANTED (Kevin Lima), THE BRAVE ONE (Neil Jorden),
PRIDE AND GLORY (Gavin O'Connor), AUGUST RUSH (KirstenSheridan), RENT (Chris Columbus),
ACROSS THE UNIVERSE (Julie Taymor), THE INTERPRETER (Sidney Pollack), FREEDOMLAND (Joe Roth),
ANALYZE THAT (Harold Ramis), WINTER PASSING (Adam Rapp), SHE HATE ME (Spike Lee), HITCH (Andy Tennant),
HOUSE OF D (David Duchovny), ANGELS IN AMERICA (Mike Nichols), TWO WEEKS NOTICE (Marc Lawrence),
UNFAITHFUL (Adrian Lyne), RIDING IN CARS WITH BOYS (Penny Marshall), MIDNIGHT COWBOY (John Schlesinger),
PENN AND TELLER GET KILLED (Arthur Penn), YOU'RE A BIG BOY NOW (Francis Ford Coppola),
BEER LEAGUE (Frank Sebastiani), THE GROOMSMEN (Edward Burns), GARDENER OF EDEN (Kevin Connelly*)*,
ONE LAST THING (Alex Steyermark), FACE (Alice Wu), IT RUNS IN THE FAMILY (Fred Schepisi),

TELEVISION (BACKGROUND)
KNIGHTS OF PROSPERITY, WITHOUT A TRACE, THE SOPRANOS, SIX DEGREES, LAW & ORDER,
L&O: SVU, L&O: CRIMINAL INTENT, THIRD WATCH, SEX AND THE CITY, RESCUE ME, NY 70 (Pilot),
THE JURY, CONVICTION, 100 CENTER STREET, BIG APPLE, DEADLINE, AS THE WORLD TURNS

TELEVISION (with PDQ Bach – see Touring below)
PDQ BACH IN HOUSTON, TONIGHT SHOW WITH JOHNNY CARSON, SMOTHERS BROTHERS COMEDY HOUR,
MIKE DOUGLAS, DAVID FROST, EVENING AT POPS, DICK CAVETT, DISNEY CHANNEL

TOURING
PDQ BACH - *Sidekick/Straightman/Stooge* - National, New York, Europe. (Grammy Winner, 1990 - 1993)

COMMERCIALS
HP/TOYS "R" US: "Stuffed Geoffrey" - *Background* -Goodby, Silverstein & Partners
COORS ORIGINAL BEER: "Sir Charles Rap" - *Biker* - Fote Cone Belding (Spike Lee)
WOOLITE: "It's a Live Blouse!" - *Puppeteer* - Cunningham & Walsh

SKILLS AND HOBBIES
Drive Anything (Except Motorcycle and 18 Wheeler), Flight Training (Piper Cherokee), Bicycle,
Roller Skate (No Rollerblades), Razor Scooter, Water Ski, Ballroom Dancing, Cooking, Bartender, Artist,
Computer (DOS, Windows), Photography, Electronics, Carpentry, Scene Painting, Scene Design,
Lighting, Stage Managing, Directing, Videography (VHS, 8mm, DV), Video/Film Editing (Premiere, Avid),
DJ, NYC Tour Guide (Licensed), NBC Guest Relations Staff (Guide and Studio Page).

Melisa Breiner-Sanders
www.MelisaBS.com

Melisa Breiner-Sanders

www.MelisaBS.com

Height – 5'2"
Hair – Blonde
Eyes – Grey

Reel and Voiceover Demo available upon request

Film / TV

Women's Studies	Beth (Lead)	Ningen Manga Productions
Blood Brothers	Lisa (Lead)	Sunjada Films
Love Knot	Angie (Lead)	Jarryd Meyer Productions
Talk Messy to Me	Woman (Lead)	Tara's Comedy Cosmos
Holler Creek Canyon	Bree (Lead)	Capital Films Studios
Intersecting Truths	Tyler (Lead)	Allbe Media Productions
Going Home	Allison (Lead)	INH Productions
Life's Short	Jill (Supporting)	INH Productions
Fighting Words	Liza "Deathblow" Stauton (Lead)	Oozing Sarcasm Productions

Theatre

InterFaith Christmas Show	Multiple parts	Punch59 Sketch Comedy (NYC)
Its All Goode	Dani's Worst Birthday	Reality Aside/Laugh Factory
Happy Hour	Flavor Wheel	M. Checkov Theatre Co (NYC)
The Women	Miriam	Tapestry Theatre Company
Cinderella	Matilda (Stepsister)	Elden Street Players
Baby with the Bathwater	Angela and Susan	Didactic Theatre Company
Vinegar Tom	Joan Noakes and Ensemble	GU, Program in Performing Arts
The Laramie Project	Reggie Fluty, Catherine Connolly, Zubaida Ula, others and Ensemble	GU, Nomadic Theatre

Training and Education

Georgetown University – BA Psychology, Theatre minor, Inter-Arts minor
Acting – Georgetown University – Prof. Karen Berman, Prof. Maya Roth, Prof. Sarah Marshall
On Camera Acting – National Conservatory for Dramatic Arts – John Vreeke
Improvisation – Georgetown University – Prof. Karen Berman, Prof. Maya Roth

Special Skills

Languages – Spanish with native accent (Spain)
Dialects – Southern US, "Redneck", Midwest US, British (Learn additional dialects quickly)
Sports – Yoga, Pilates, Kickboxing, Horseback Riding, Billiards, Bowling, Running
Dance – Minimal Tap (have tap shoes), Minimal Jazz, Club
Other – Licensed Driver, Current Passport, Teacher, Photography, Lisp, Impersonation/Imitation

STEVE REILLY

STEVE REILLY

Born - July 4. Raised on Vashon Island in Puget Sound.
Began acting locally as a child in Kindergarten, Grade
School, Junior High, & High School.
Graduated from Vashon High School.
Graduated from Central Washington University - Theatre &
Drama & Special Education.
Attended Earl Kelly's "Director's School of Acting" - Moore
Theatre, Seattle Wa.
Character Acting throughout school, Community Theatre and
University.
Drama Director (17 years) - Eisenhower High School
(Yakima, Wa.)
Past board member - Washington Interscholastic Activities
Association
Past President - Washington Alliance for Theatre Education
Past board member - Warehouse Community Theatre -
Yakima, Wa.
Former overnight DJ - KATS FM (Yakima, Wa.)
Stagehand, Stage Manager, Promoter Rep. - MCA Concerts
& "The Gorge" (Wa.)
Appear in 2007 music video "The Rifle" by Alela Diane
Appear in 2007 short film "The Rifle Workbook" by Vincent
Caldoni.
Prefer to act in film "character" roles in Pacific Northwest.
At present time - Retired

Edward
Morris
Rollin

Edward Morris Rollin

SAG / AFTRA

Web site: www.EdwardMorrisRollin.com   IMDb credits

Film	Role	Director
AFTERWARDS	Paramedic	Gilles Bourdos
NEVER FOREVER	Waiter	Gina Kim
AS GOOD AS IT GETS	Roy (scene w/ Jack Nicholson)	James Brooks
GARDEN STATE	Hardware store salesman	Zach Braff
PARTY MONSTER	NYPD Police Officer	F. Bailey & Randy Barbato
SHELTER (shelterthemovie.com)	Nosey neighbor	Benno Shoberth
COOKING FOR RICHARD	Frank	Ido Fluk
BUSH	Solo	Freeland Shreve
DOUBLE-U	Mr. W	Laurent Notaro
JOHNNY MONTANA	Lucarelli (FDNY Paramedic)	John Daniel Gavin
NINE OUT OF TEN	Officer Tittle	Orson Cummings

Television

CHAPPELLE'S SHOW ("Legal Systems")	Corrections Officer	Rusty Cundieff
UNSOLVED MYSTERIES	Businessman	Eric Taylor
REAR WINDOW	Oxygen tank delivery man (scene w/ Christopher Reeve)	Jeff Bleckner

Theatre

MANHATTAN MONOLOGUE SLAM	Various	Bowery Poetry Club
POLARIS NORTH REPERTORY	Various	NYC
EDDY ROLLIN ENSEMBLE	Musician / Singer	Knitting Factory, CBGB's etc.
THEATRE OF THE ABSURD	Comedic characters	La Mama, NYC
BEYOND THERAPY	Bruce	Somers Playhouse, NY
ORPHANS	Philip	Somers Playhouse, NY

Commercials / Voice Overs

Conflicts available upon request.

Training

Scene Study	William Hickey	H.B. Studios
Commercials	Jerry Coyle	Weist-Barron
Improvisation	Thomas Sodder	Group Sessions
Bachelor Of Fine Arts	Music	California Institute Of The Arts

Special Skills   *(Valid US Passport).
Precision driver (stick), Musician / Conductor; Teacher; Clown (juggle); Dancer; Photographer; Stock Broker; Mover; Truck Driver; Mechanic; Carpenter; Fisherman; Licensed Real Estate Broker; Lifeguard; Astronomer, Chef, Yoga, Tai Chi.

Accents / Character Voices
New York tough guy; Brooklyn; Jewish Immigrant; Southern; Falsetto (imitate children); Fake languages; (Russian), Alien; Imitate animals; Vocalization improvisation; Cartoon Characters; Bird calls.

Musical Instruments / Vocal Range: Baritone *View music credits: www.EddyRollin.com
Saxophone (Soprano, Alto, Tenor), Oboe, Oboe d'Amore, English Horn, Clarinet, Recorder, Bass Guitar, Percussion, Keyboard, Ethnic Double Reeds, Harmonica, invented instruments (Giraffe Horn, Twanger, Angel Harp).

Sports
Softball, Basketball, Tennis, Badminton, Ping Pong, Frisbee, Pool, Boating, Swimming, Snorkle, Golf, Horseback riding.

James "The Glow" Goff

GOT GLOW?
PRODUCTIONS

BIO

Born and raised in the South Bronx, James "The Glow" Goff is a shining star to look out for. The Glow started his career when, through the advice of friend, he decided to give it a try.

In just a couple of years in the business, James Goff had already made the transition from "up and coming" to comedian by opening for comedian greats such as Tommy Davidson, DL Hughley, and "TourGasm" stars Robert Kelly, Gary Gulman, & Jay Davis.

He was also a Boston regional finalist for Comedy Central's "Open Mic Fight". With all these credits to his resume, he still has time to perform in top comedy clubs all across the New England and Tri state area.

When asked to describe his brand of comedy, James Goff just simply states, "truth meets therapy." The Glow's stage presence alone reminds you of the greats before him. With his trademark glowing smile and his insight on the world around him, you see why audiences love him. It's safe to say that James "The Glow" Goff is one of the bright faces in the future of comedy.

ACCOLADES:
2007 Regional Finalist in Comedy Central's Open Mic Fight

LYLE BEGAYE

LYLE BEGAYE

LOCATION: Los Angeles, CA AGE: 31
HEIGHT: 5' 10   HAIR: Black
WEIGHT: 158   EYES: Brown
SHIRT: 16   SUIT : 0
WAIST: 32   SHOE: 10
INSEAM: 40   ETHNICITY: Native American

FILM:
Never acted before, but I want to try and get into the movies though!

TELEVISION:
Never acted before, but being on a sitcom wouldn't hurt either!

THEATER:
None Yet

COMMERCIALS:
Hopefully I'll land a gig real soon!

MODELING:
If someone would give me a chance, then we'll go from there!

TRAINING:
Went to a little bit of acting school for Elizabeth Savage Talent/ Jonathan Minks was
my teacher. He did thus a many roles in movies and extras here and there.

SPECIAL SKILLS:
Playing basketball, lifting weights, bowling, certified bartender, rock climbing, running,
bike riding, little bit of hip hop dancing, two-step country western dancing.

Seymour M. Horowitz

Seymour Horowitz   AFTRA SAG AEA

Ht: 6'1"   Wt: 250#   Eyes: Brown   Hair: Bald (S&P)   Age: 65-75

Films, TV (include)	**Day Player**	**(Videotape available)**
The Replacements *	Gangster	Warner Bros.
The Surprise Party *	Short Order Cook	Expedition Films
Statue of Liberty *	Reporter	NBC TV
Homicide *	Medical Examiner	NBC TV
Nightowls of Coventry *	Marv (lead) **	Nightowl Prods.
Countdown to Looking Glass*	Father	HBO TV
The Net	Fruit Peddler	Paramount
Minority Report	Father	20th Century
Going Home to Bklyn	Self (lead)	HGTV
Unsolved Mysteries	Mob Boss	NBC TV
Hawk	Landlord	ABC TV
America's Most Wanted	Witness	Fox TV

* listed <IMDB.com>   ** <nightowls of coventry.> (google)

Commercials(include)	**Principal Player**	**(CD available)**
NYC Lottery	Old Russian	NYC ;TriState
7 On Your Side	Mr. Cheetum	Channel 7 DC
Mash's Ham	Mr. Salt	Regional TV
1st American Bank	Executive	Regional TV
Mattress Discounters	Husband	Regional TV
Political Spots	Various	Regional TV
Pharmaceutical	Mechanic	National TV

Stage (includes)	**Professional**	**(AEA since 1962)**
A Rosen By Any Other Name	Ardenshensky	Center Stage VA
Cantorial	Morris	Center Stage VA
Picasso at Lapin Agile	Gaston	CharlotteRep NC
Cemetery Club	Sam Katz	Jupiter Tht'r FL
As You Like It	Duke Frederick	Shakspr Park DC
The Odd Couple	Murray the Cop	VillaRosa MD
Plaza Suite	(3) Male Leads	Fairlingtn VA
Golden Fleecing	Pete Dilucca	Old Globe SD CA
Children of Darkness	Jonathan Wilde	Old Globe SD CA
The Visit	Police Chief	Studio Thtr DC
Vatzlav	Gen.Barbarro	W.MammothDC
Guys & Dolls	NathanDetroit	SmithsonianDC
Zorba the Greek	Zorba	Cedar Knoll VA
Paint Your Wagon	Ben Rumsen	LubberRun VA
Gypsy	Herbie	Gateway Bellport.
Oklahoma	Ali Hakem	" " Bellpurt,LI

can walk to Silvercup and Kaufman Studios
Vessel Docked in East River

for
Commercial
Bookings

**Rita Frazier
AFTRA - SAG**
For more pix
& IMDB credits
www.RitaNYC.us

www.PostcardsR.Us collector series

Rita Frazier, AFTRA - SAG
www.RitaNYC.us

was recently submitted for a
Heineken Commercial
through www.Bgroundinc.com

Avaialble for
AFTRA-SAG Commercial
& Skits

Can walk to Silvercup and
Kaufman Studios

www.PhotosNYC.com

www.PostcardsR.Us Collector Series

Chocolate
Milk

Missing

From Current Commercials
Rita Frazier, AFTRA - SAG

for Commercials Bookings

For more
and
IMDB cre
www.RitaN

Rita Frazier

AFTRA # 7615   SAG # 91056

Commercials 2006:
None at press time

Trade Shows/Product Demoes:
Proctor-Silex   Wear-Ever
Cuisinart etc.
in Chicago (Housewares Show), New York State Fair,
Atlantic City (Home Ec Show), NYC, etc.

Special Abilities:
New York City Police Department
June 2000 Citizens' Police Academy Graduate
EMT [Emergency Medical Technician] Training 1986
9-1-1 Dispatching film set consultant 1986
Taught CPR with Ambulance Corps 1986
Disaster scene training 1986
Professional Level Free-Style Dancing

Bonus:
Book Rita as an EMT and she can help set-up the
scene to assure medical authenticity.

Specifications:
Age Range 47 to 61
Height   5'5"
Weight   220 Lbs
Bust   40-C
Waist   44
Hips   46 3/4
Dress   18-20
Hair   Reddish Brown
Eyes   Brown
Passport   USA

Film & Television:
Dave Chappelle DVD Season 1 Episode #108
talking about *Mr Ed the Taking Horse*

Paramedic/Emergency Medical Technician in;
"NYPD Blue"
and many other productions

Medical Examiner in;
"America's Most Wanted"

Nurse in:
"Requiem for a Dream"
Gave Ellen Burstyn the KNOCKOUT shot
and many other productions

Stage:
Subject for major illusions 1986, e.g.:
Houdini Blade Box
Beheading, etc.

Wardrobe Owned: *
1 Emergency Medical Technician (EMT)
-with props *
classic white & green with badge or navy *
2 Operating Room Scrub Set (head to toe) *
3 NYS Court Room Officer *
4 Doctor (ward, ER, etc.) -with props *
5 Lab Technician *

* Partner to match above available

6 Nurse (regular and pediatric nurse)
7 Waitress
8 Church Lady (Deaconess/Choir Member)
9 Formal wear

171

DEANNA
CHARETT.

174

DeAnna Charett

Website: http://imdb.com/name/nm2397201/

Build: Medium, Athletic Hair: Lt Brown
Height: 5' 8 ½" Eyes: Hazel
Location: Baton Rouge, La

FILM

Major Movie Star	Supporting role	Steve Miner/
Millenium Films		
Telephone Book	Supporting role	AlanWooley/
WooleyEntertainment		

INTERNET

The Black Ghost	Recurring role	Will Warner/
I.C.E. Studios		

COMMERCIAL
List upon Request

ON SET EXPERIENCE
Kissing Frogs / DMS, LLC / Production Assistant / Lana Roberts

TRAINING
TVI STUDIOS: Film & Television Industry Intensive, TVI Studios (Los Angeles, Ca)
DAVE ORNSTON: The Audition Workshop
LANCE NICHOLS: Film Technique , Auditioning for Film and Television
VELEKA GRAY: Advanced classes: Stage to Screen, Audition, Succeed in Show Biz, In Depth
Scene Study , Acting for Film, On Camera Acting, Movement in Action, Incorporating Action in
Scenes, Accessing Actors' Emotions

SPECIAL SKILLS
Martial Arts: Over 15 years in TaeKwonDo; 4th Degree Black Belt, 2003 Bronze Medalist at the
29th U.S. National TaeKwonDo Championships, Proficient with Kamas, Sword, Bo Staff and
Escrima Sticks.
Military: Over 19 years in the U.S. Armed Forces, Sergeant in the U.S. Army Reserves, 10
years in the U.S. Air Force, Sharpshooter & Marksman with M-16 rifle. 8 ½ years as a Graphic
Illustrator.
Other skills: 3 years as a Casino Dealer, Learning Russian and Korean.

J. Michael Ferniany

J. MICHAEL FERNIANY
SAG/AFTRA/AEA

Ht: 5'7"   Hair: Black/gray
Wt. 175 lbs   Eyes: Brown

Film:

Credits (partial list)	Role:	Director:
Holy Cannoli	Carlo	B. Bhargava (Unexposed Prods.)
The Price	Mr. Rossi	Abel Gonzalez (168 Film Festival)
Who's Next	Professor	Zeus Quijano (U.S.C.)
Smoke Screen	Joe	J. J. Papillier (SAG Indie.)
Rectuma	Summa Cum Lauden	M. Pirro (Pirromount)
Howie	Shlomo	Angelo Mei (Art. Inst. L.A.)
Sub Rosa	Hank	Tanner Madix (A.V.P.A.)
Locked Out	Bob (lead)	Marc Bethke (N.Y. Film)
Sonata For Dani	Shawn	Yash Herrington (L.M.U.)

Television:

Price of a Broken Heart	John	Paul Shapiro (Lifetime)
The Golden Girls	George	Paul Bogart (NBC)
Benson	William	Bill Foster (ABC)
It's A Living	Frankie	Joel Zwick (ABC)
Soap	Jesse	Jay Sandrich (ABC)

Theatre:

The Leaning Tree	Abe Fazrunner	The Complex Theatre
Trolls	Juan	Coast Playhouse
American Iliad	Clyde Tolson	Victory Theatre
The Rothschilds	Prince Metternick	Jewish Theatre South
Anyone Can Whistle	Cookie	Dupree Theatre
Mandragola	Friar Timoteo	Off Ramp Theatre
ANZAC I & II	Henry	Globe Playhouse
Magdalene	Asbadar	Coast Playhouse
Sparkles	Bob/Braum	Coast Playhouse
Scapino!	Sylvestro	Agape Theatre
You're A Good Man, Charlie Brown	Snoopy	Academy Theatre
The Pajama Game	Max	Los Feliz Theatre
Presto! A Magic Show	Clown/Mime	Alliance Theatre

Training:

Cold Reading Technique	Craig Wallace	SAG Conservatory
Acting Technique	L. A. City College	Cliff O'Connell
Transpersonal Acting	Workshop	Ned Mandarino
Scene Study	Van Mar Academy	Ivan Markota &SMC/B.Gannen
Voice and Diction	Lee Strasberg Institute	Marge Haber
Commercial Acting	Watkins Commercials	George Watkins
Private Vocal Training	Margery Anwyl	Harold Brown/Seth Riggs
Musical Theatre (Dramatic Baritone)	L. A. City College	Mel Dancill/John Ingle
Jazz/Tap	Rainbow Studios	Lee Carter
Dialects (French/Italian/Cockney	Spanish/Southern	George Gilbert
Speech Major	Auburn University (B.A.)	University of Alabama (M.A.)

Reviews: "Osama look alike (J. Michael Ferniany) provides a choice capper as the suicide bomber who gets Rectuma where it hurts." Variety – "Rectuma"

Eric Kaldor

ERIC KALDOR
SAG

HT: 5'10"   WT: 150   Hair: Grey   Eyes: Blue

Television

Building History	Supporting	History Channel
Untold Stories From the E.R.	Featured	TLC
Guilty or Innocent	Featured (2)	Discovery
Family Business	Guest Star (3)	Showtime
The Guiding Light	Recurring	CBS
The Mind of Man	Recurring	PBS
The Stranger	Featured	ABC
Kojak	Recurring	CBS
The Hostage Heart	Featured	ABC
When the Whistle Blows	Featured	NBC

Film

Truth, Justice, and The American Way	Supporting	Paramount
National Lampoon's Secret Video	Supporting	ASProductions
National Lampoon's Secret Videos II	Supporting	ASProductions
The Man With Bogart's Face	Supporting	Paramount
Silverman	Supporting	Alliance
Aaron Loves Angela	Supporting	Columbia

Theatre

Ogunquit Playhouse	Various	Various
Milk and Honey (B'way – 1 yr)	Art	Bill Appel
Walkup (Off B'way)	Jack	Matt Zimber
We Americans (revival B'way)	Leon	Luther Adler
The Iceman Cometh	Barney	Jose Quintero

Training
Uta Hagen-Herbert Berghoff Studios, N.Y.C.
Diane Castle Workshop, LA
Carolyne Barry Commercial Workshop, L.A.

Skills
Fluent French, Body Building, Yoga, Long Distance Swimming
Dialects: New Yorkese, French, Southern

USHASI KITCHEN

USHASI KITCHEN

CAREER OBJECTIVE :
To work in the Entertainment Industry as a Model / Acting.

I have dreamed of being a Model/Actress since I was a Lady.
I got married , having kids and raised family, never got to pursue that dream.
Now, I think its time for me to go on with my life and do something I would enjoy.

I have no professional experience of doing "Modeling" /" Acting " in Entertainment Industry at all. But I am very much interested in learning more.
I would love to be an " Extra " or "Model" or anything in the Movie Industry, love being around people.

I think this is a great opportunity for me, I look forward for great experiences through this industry and what they have to offer, greatly appreciated.

To get my face exposed Acting is somethingI wanted to do my entire life, never had a chance.

I love to play all types of characters.

I could be sweet and innocent looking OR naughty and sexy looking.

I feel I was born to entertain people and that's exactly what I am trying to do.
I hope its not too late.

thank you.

USHASI

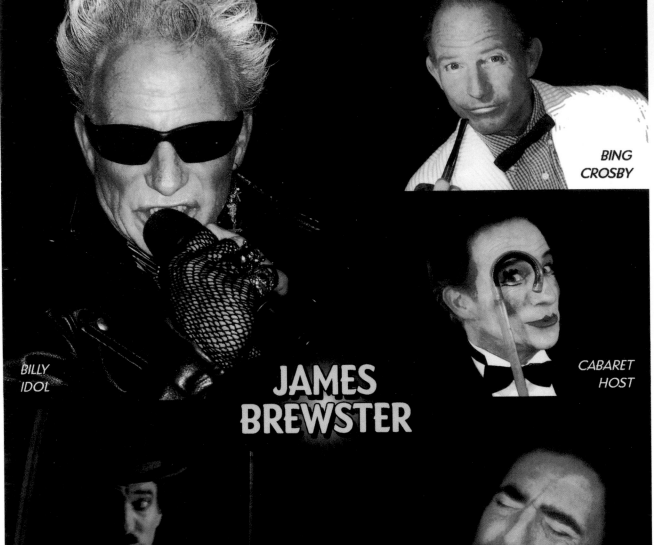

BING
CROSBY

BILLY
IDOL

JAMES
BREWSTER

CABARET
HOST

CHARLIE
CHAPLIN

CAPT. JACK
SPARROW

NEAL
DIAMOND

James Brewster
AFTRA/SAG

Height: 5'8
Weight: 155
Hair: Brown
Eyes: Hazel

TELEVISION

Citizen Boss	US Congressman Rudy	Russian TV/ Etalon Film Production
Forensic Files	Nathan Allen	Court TV
Forensic Files	Richard Van Dusen	Court TV
One Life To Live	Under 5	ABC

FILM

Maniac	principal	Joe Spinel, Magnum Motion Pictures
The Deadly Spawn	Sam (principal)	Bohus Production
Vigilante	Bobby	Magnum Motion Pictures
Jim's Movie	Jim	Van Brunt Film Production
One World Trade Center	Cliff (lead)	Independent short

WEBCAST

Aid To Andorra	Deputy Secretary Paul Heffron	www.onion.com

THEATER

Counting The Ways	He	Edward Albee-director- NAC NYC
That Championship Season	Coach	National Arts Club NYC
Twelve Angry Men	Juror No. Three	National Arts Club NYC
The Dinner Party	Andre Bouville	National Arts Club NYC
Jack and Shirley	Jack	La MaMa E.T.C. NYC
William's Last Chance	William Joist	Third Avenue Productions
No Way To Treat A Lady	Det. Morris Brummell	Edison Valley Playhouse
One Flew Over The Cuckoo's Nest	Randle P. McMurphy	Edison Valley Playhouse
Blood Brothers	Narrator	Edison Valley Playhouse
42nd St.	Julian Marsh	Cranford Repertory Company
The King And I	King	Cranford Repertory Company

SINGING

A Tribute to the Rat Pack	Frank Sinatra	NY Dinner Theater
Celebrity Impersonations	Frank Sinatra, Neil Diamond, Bing Crosby, Capt. Jack Sparrow, Charlie Chaplin	Celebrity Reviews, private, club, Corporate events
Just Havin' Fun	Writer/producer/performer	Cabaret theater-to-go
KALEB	Lead singer/songwriter/rhythm guitarist	Christian rock act
Return To Romance	Lead singer	Jazz/pop Quintet

TRAINING

Michael Howard Studios NYC	Scene Study	Polina Klimovitskaya
The Film Acting Studio NYC	On-Camera-Scene Study, Cold Reading	Jeffrey Stocker

Skills

Guitar, drums, percussion, songwriting/production, equestrian (English & Western), golf, tennis, baseball, volleyball, surfing, kayaking, pool, ping-pong **SPECIAL SKILLS** Fire-eating, broad sword combat

Sabrina Mason

Sabrina Mason
Non-Union

HEIGHT: **5' 8"**
WEIGHT: **130**
HAIR: **Honey Blonde**
EYES: **Brown**

THEATER: No Experience yet.

TV/FILM: Movie "The Cost Of Family" Shooting Memphis, TN. (2008) Lead
            Role (Justina)
            Film "Radio Free Albemuth" Shooting Los Angeles, CA. (2007) Extra
            Role (Prisoner)

COMMERCIAL: Radio Commercials Only – Cold Reads

TRAINING: WHGM Radio Station – Savannah, GA.

MODELING: Fashion and Runway experience since 2005. New York City – Photo
            Shoot, July 2007.

SPECIAL SKILLS: Computer literate, Background Singing, Fashion,
Speed Reading, Modeling, Managing, Secretarial, and Organizational. Clothing
Boutique owner.

Chester Dale

CHESTER DALE

S.A.G. & A.F.T.R.A

Featured roles (partial list)

2007	Revolution	Kathy Fitzgerald	Lead role French mercenary for US revolution	Francois
2006	To The Tranquil Sea	Steven Parkhurst	scruffy, Russian assassin "Sargeant"	Yuri
2006	Adventures Of Stanley Stranger: The Deep End	J. L. Taylor uncaring, gruff		Pa
2006	Absent Father	Allison Sherman. High school history instructor		Mr. Ramis
2006	In The Professor's Class	Rachel Israel. Philosophy instructor	Professor Jameson	
2006	Emily's Problem	George Olken. unconcerned, egotistic downstairs neighbor		Elliott
2006	Erie Road	Michael Weinstein. senior forensic pathologist	Doctor Giddle	
2005	Trust	Ashley Mueller. the secretive & creepy shopkeeper		Hiram
2005	Film Camp: Reel One	Garret Maynard. obnoxious	Paparazzo Photographer	
2005	The Namesake	Mira Nair. unreasonably demanding	American Obstetrician	
2005	The Bamboo Shark	Dennis Ward. nasty, threatening	M.I.T. Dean Of Housing	
2004	John And Abigail Adams	Peter Jones US constitution signer	John Dickenson	
2003	A Thing About My Folks	Raymond DeFilitta gas-station grease-monkey		Bill
2003	Long Hard Road To Freedom	Ronald Howard. angry	William Lloyd Garrison	
2001	Kate And Leopold	James Mangold. upstairs	Butler and Leopold's Dresser	
1997	Amistad	Steven Spielberg. State Representative and	Town Cryer	

Assorted roles in over 75 features, student /deferred-pay experimental films or television shows
Various print & television ads and naturally, conflicts available upon request

Skills and Abilities:

ocean-crossing sailing yachts' navigation & racing, SCUBA, rowing, canoe, shell, kayak, spelunking, simple archery, bowling, bicycling, judo, free- weight and nautilus weightlifting, fencing epee and saber, rock-climbing. bulldozer, crane, forklift, chainsaw, assorted farm, construction, factory & office machines. I am quite comfortable with large and small animals. 5'11" 190 lbs. nude model. current passport, rifle & handgun license face-cast & voice disk available.

Voices: baritone singing voice, speak French. assorted British-empire and trans-Europe voices, and various English- speaking African and Indian peoples' accents

I Own: 8 business suits, 4 differently-styled black tuxedoes, black "tails", white tuxedo, 150 new & old men's ties, doctor's scrubs, derelict/street- scum-bag clothes, 1700's gent's outfit, assorted older-styled eyeglasses, older-styled leather attaché cases, wigs, yachting foul-weather gear, simple and compound target- bows, ocean-going shell, x-c skis, butterfly net, scythe, assorted hand- tools, assorted equipment for SCUBA, backpacking, sailing, gardening, cooking.

Also an Immaculately kept 1977 Mercedes 450 SEL and 1993 Honda Civic (pictures available)

Sizes: 42Reg. Suit, 16 ½-34 Shirt, 35W-33L Trousers, 9 ½ Shoes, 8 ½ Glove, 7 3/4 Hat

It is said that I look like: William Lloyd Garrison or actors William Hurt, Christopher Lloyd, James Woods, Ron Howard, physicist Doron Weber, sports guys Terry Bradshaw & Peter Bethune, Seth Thomas, Rembrandt Peale and an assortment of historical WASP, yankee types

Schools:

Moravian College	B.S.	Pre-Psychiatric Medicine
Computer Processing Institute	(cert.)	Small Business Computing Systems
Porter and Chester Institute	(cert.)	Computer-Aided Drafting -Architecture
Lady Cyana Dive School	(cert.)	PADI Advanced Open Water SCUBA
J-World Sailing School	(cert.)	advanced sail- racing techniques
Norwalk Community College		on-camera acting techniques
Cablevision offices	(cert.)	community equipment usage

TONY DADIKA

TONY DADIKA

AEA, AFTRA

FILM (FEATURE)

"Silent"	Mr.Archibald	Lead	Dir. M. Pleckaitis
"Anything For You"	Dr. Miller	Supporting	Dir. A. Alagappan
"Cluster"	Mr. Winters	Supporting	Dir. V. Scordia
"Methodic"	Sr. Det. Dan Grant	Secondary	Dir Chris Notarile
"Seesaw"	Senior Doorman	Supporting	Dir. Tom Muschamp
"Between 2 Evils"	Tom Ward	Secondary	Dir J.B.Nelson
"What Realy Frightens You?"	Officer York	Supporting	Dir. R. W.Haines
"Sordid Things	Judge Miller	Supporting	Dir A. Blumenthal
"Book of truth Book of Lies"	Detective Jones	Supporting	Dir M. Dvortov
"Teshuvah"	Judge Ramos	Supporting	Dir A Weston
"Monocerus"	Police Officer	Supporting	Dir. Adam Martin
"Playing Doctor"	Police Officer	Supporting	Dir. J. Banks
"Man Push Cart"	Cart cusromer	Supporting	Dir. Ramin Bahrimin

FILM (SHORT)

"The Cabinet"	Dr Caligari	Lead	Dir. Chris Notarile
"Redimere"	Father McDaniels	Supporting	Dir. Cesar Cruz
"Mom vs The Undead"	Zombie	Supporting	Dir. James Darling
'Axe Massacre	Gus	Lead	Dir Chris R. Notarile
"The Prowler"	Sal Monaco	Secondary	Dir Chris R. Notarile
"Blue Beetle" (trailer)	Jarvis Kord	Lead	Dir. Chris R. Notarile
"The Protector"	Old Protector	Lead	Dir. Chris R. Notarile
"The Hit"(trailer)	Tony Vivaldi	Secondary	Dir. Chris R .Notarile
"Underneath It All"	Officer Dolan	Supporting	Dir. Lance J Reah
"Exit Irak"	U.S. Army Line General	Supporting	Dir. Michael Andrew
"Crude"'	Dick Cheney	Secondary	Dir. G. Smith
"D4 Delivery"	Stan	Supporting	Dir. Heylan Lee

TELEVISION

"Southern Gothic" (pilot)	Abe Vickers	Lead	Dir M.A. Gutman
"Tony & Shlomoh Show"	Host	Lead	Dir. Anthony Dadika
"Parco PI	Boris Navinsky	U-5	Mark Mark Prod. CRTV
"Knight Rider (pilot)	Devon Miles	Lead	Goolaplang Prod.(Tialar
"PR" (Gone To Far) (pilot)	Cuddy	Secondary	Dir Wendy M Jean
"spy Games" (Timley Visit)	Head Waiter	U-5	BIZZ TV (Russia)

SPECIAL TALENTS

Artist, photographer, golfer, skydiver, fisherman, soccer coach ,basketball coach, softball coach, writer draftsman, carpenter, ,corporate executive, graphic artist, cook, speak conversational Russian.

TRAINING

School For Film & Television - William Paterson University - Donna Marrazzo - TVI commercial Judy Bowman

Cindy Stauffer

Cindy Stauffer Non-Union

Hair Color: Blonde
Eye Color: Blue
Height: 5'4"

FILM

Trio	extra	Trio Productions

TV

Bangor Halloween Parade	Co-host	Service Electric TV
Channel 69 News	Guest	Channel 69

COMMERCIAL

B104 Makeover Contest	Morning Show Co-host	B104
B104 Morning Show	Co-host	B104

VOICEOVER

Straub Chrysler Jeep	Main
WLEV Christmas	woman opening presents
WLEV Christmas	drunk
Kay Jewelers	Main

THEATER

Tidings	Honi	Pennsylvania Playhouse
Godspell	Sonia	Cedar Crest Stage
Anything Goes	Hope	Pennsylvania Playhouse
Medea	Medea	Cedar Crest Stage
Snoopy	Peppermint Patty	Shepherd Hills Theater
The Grapes of Wrath	Agnes	Civic Theater
A Funny Thing Happened On the Way to the Forum	Geminae	Shepherd Hills Theater

PRINT

Lehigh Valley Style

LIVE EVENT/PROMOTION

Miss Pennsylvania Scholarship Pageant	Emcee
Musikfest	Host/Singer
Mayfair	Host/Singer
Flyers Skate Zone Grand Opening	Host
Kidsfest	Host

TRAINING

Weist Barron Commercial Training
Civic Theater Theater School
Muhlenberg College Theater Workshop
DeSales University Theater Student
Cedar Crest College Theater Student
StageDoor Workshop
Private acting coaching with Joan Barber

SPECIAL SKILLS

Improvisation	18 years voice training	horseback riding
audience interaction	jazz dance	volleyball
radio broadcasting	ballet	swimming
commercial writing	tap	
	ballroom	

SPECIAL SKILLS: LANGUAGE

Southern
Cockney

SPECIAL SKILLS: OTHER

makes balloon animals
eye for fashion and decorating
always current on celebrity news
loves animals
loves children
Waitressing
drives manual transmission
knowledge of construction
uses power tools

Shelly Morgan

Merry Christmas

Bio:

I was a Santa at St. Dominic School for exceptional children for 10 years.
I have retired my reindeer for a hybrid sleigh.
Yours
Santa Shelly

Karen Paolini

Karen Paolinl

Hair: Strawberry Blonde   Height: 5'3"   Eyes: Hazel   Weight 120 lbs

Film:

The Ones You Love	Billy's Mom	NYFA. Danile D. Director, NY, NY
Eastside Story	Mother	United Films, Bronx, NY
Demolition Man	Jhade	Alex Diaz, Director, NJ
Peach Martini Series	Alta	Kirk Bowman Director, LA, CA
50 Ways to Lose Your Lover	Party Girl Earthquake	Spelling Productions, LA,CA
Only in Hollywood	Homeless	Cherish Michael Productions, LA,CA
Nellie Furtado Music Video	NF Stand In	Dreamworks, Univereal City, LA, CA

Television:

Playboy 50th Anniversary	Contestant	Playboy TV, North Hollywood, CA
Jimmy Kimmel Show	Dating Contestant	Jimmy Kimmel Productions, LA,CA
Judge Joe Brown	Plaintiff	Judge Joe Productions, LA,CA

Theatre:

The March	Letta	Florence Miils, Director, NY, NY
Floating Island Monologue	Sophia	Brief Acts Company, NY, NY
Happy Hour	Beat Up	Mike Horn Director, NY, NY
Tales of the Black Veil 5	Vampiress	Rod Barnes, Dlrector, NY, NY
Ragtime	Bridgitt, ensemble	Heights Players, Brooklyn, NY
Midsummer in Mexico	Understudy	True North Ensemble, NY, NY
Aesop	Understudy	Cube City Entertainment, NY, NY
Far Side of Paradise	Diane	TSI/Playtime Series, NY, NY
Antigone	Euridice	Theatre Ssn Greal, Sl, NY
Prometheus	Rhea	Theatre San Greal, SI, NY
Medea	Old Woman	Theatre San Gred, Sl, NY
Everything in the Carden	Mrs. Toothie	Pasadena School of Art & Design,CA
Rain	Islander	Kentwood Players, CA (rehearsals only)
Spooky House	Witch	SH Productions, Ventura, CA
Studio City Holiday Parade	Mrs. Claus	Studio City COC,CA
Queen Mary Shipwreck 2002	Ghost - guillotine	Shipwreck Productions, LB, CA
The King & I	Wife / Dancer	Navdancer Prod., Ventura, CA
Happy Anniversary Angel!	Arlene-Press Agent	Eastern Boys Cabaret Prod., Orange, CA
Cyranno De Bergerac	Duenna, Marguerite	Camarillo Theatre, Camarillo, CA
Queen Mary Shipwreck 2001	Artic Ghost	Shipwreck Prod., Long Beach, CA
World Peace Festival	Poetry "2000"	Hollywood Church of Religious Science
NY Star Pageant	Runner Up/Model	PMSP Productions, NY, NY

Radio: ARN Radio Networks - DJ - Hollywood, CA 2003
News Anchor/Reporter - CNBC Desktop News. WRUN/WKGW, SUNNY 103/WGNY, WDOS, WVOS, WZOZ.

Training: American Academy of Dramatic Arts, NY, .NY - DiCarlo, Anderson, Jensen
HB Studios, NY, NY - French, Owens
AIA Actors Studio - Burbank, CA
Actors Edge - LA, CA
Act Now, LA, CA
The Berubians - Hollywood, CA - Improvisation

Dance: Broadwav DanceCenter (NY, NY) - Ballet, Tap, Jazz
Steppes on Broadnav (NY. NY) - Jazz
SUNY Oneonta, NY - acting, ballet
Richmond Gymnastics Cenier - (SI, NY) - gmnastics, ballet
Film / Theatre / Television - Over 25 EXTRA ROLES, NY, CA, model and dancer

Larry Canady

Larry Canady

AFTRA

HEIGHT:	5'8"	**WEIGHT:**	175 lbs.
HAT:	7 ¼	**NECK:**	17
JACKET:	46	**WAIST:**	36
INSEAM:	30	**SHOES:**	9 ½

TELEVISION
The Maury Show	Slasher	WPIX
Amerika, Amerika	Morticai	Victor Pedchenko
Saving Our History FBI Stings	Thief: Ernest Medford	The History Channel
HBO Pilot	Mr. Brown	Steven Weills Prod.
Hitch	Ricky	Affiliated Films

MUSIC VIDEO
Fat Joe	Homeless	Song: "So Much More"
Cameron	FBI Agent	Rockefeller
Enrique Iglesias	'Quizas'	Interscope Records
Alicia Keys	'You Don't Know My Name'	

ON CAMERA PRINCIPAL
The Rodneys	Mr. Barnett	Linley Fawley
Half Pint	Old Man	NYU Production
Officer Training Video	Security Officer	Beggar's Row Theatre

PERFORMANCES & THEATRE
Obsession	Uncle Milton	Actor's Loft
Day Of Absence	Clem	Pratt Institute
Canterville Ghost	Timmy	American Tour
From Kite to Kiddie Hawk	Orville	Robin Hood Players
Undermilkwood	Cherry, Waldo, Child	Performing Arts
Blues for Mr. Charlie	Pete	Apollo Theatre
Rats	Baby	Theatre Interplay
Antigone	Soldier	Theatre Interplay

COMMERCIAL
Available Upon Request

TRAINING
Brooklyn College	BA Speech Communication
High School of Performing Arts	Speech, Improv, Scene Study, Sense Memory, Dance,
Madelin Burns Studio	Theatre - Sarah Stein, On Camera - John Gallagher
Creative Acting	Commercial Acting - Barry Shapiro, Scene Study - Mario
	Giacolonie, Improv - John Puglisi

SPECIAL SKILLS
Baseball, handball, boxing, jogging, singing, Drivers License: auto/shift, NYC Teacher, great with children, stand - up, photography

ACCENTS
African, Southern, Jamaican, Brooklyn

Reel Available

MISCELLANEOUS
1999 Grand Prix, business attire, tuxedo, Military (Honorable Discharged)

Liz Bauer - *Actress*

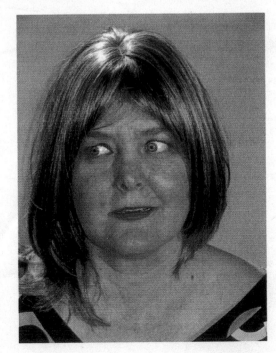

5'7
BROWN OR BLONDE HAIR

NYC STUDENT FILM DIRECTED BY JARRAH GURRIE

NATIONAL TV:
JENNY JONES SHOW CHICAGO IL, WANNA BE SUPERSTARS
SAND "CRAZY"

vIDEOS:
"TEN POUND STRIKE" NYC NY
CHRIS ALLEN   CLEVELAND OH

HOLLYWOOD MOVIE:
AWAKE OF THE DEAD BY SILVERSTORM PROD
PLAYED THE OLD LADY
MEDICAL SHOW REENACTMENTS: ECHO ENT
HAD A HEART ATTACK

LOCAL MOVIE:
MURDER MACHINE BY TWISTEDSPINE FILMS
PLAYED LIZ BI-SEXAL GIRLFRIEND
PEARLS BEFORE SWINE DIRECTED BY JOH WILHEM
BARTENDER
BAD GUY SPEAKS DIRECTED BY BRUNO TATALOVIC
HAD THE ONLY SPEAKING PART IN MOVIE
GUYS BY 216 FILMS DIRECTED BY JOE OSTRICA
BARTENDER
DONNIE BROOKS PLAYED THE GRANDFATHER GIRLFRIEND (SMOKED IN THAT SCENE
MARTIANS FROM VENUS DIRECTED BY ALAN GOULDER PLAYED THE WIFE

SPECIAL THINGS:
COOKING
BLUE BELT IN TAE KWON DO
LOVES BOXING

LEO LUNSER

Leo Lunser
Acting Resume for Film & Stage

Age:58, Height: 6'3", Weight: 208

FILM

T   C   Y   R

MOTHER MADE ME – Mystical Media Productions – 2003 (Supporting role)
THE NINE – Aranmor Productions – 2004 – (Featured role)
SALVATION – Mystical Media Productions – 2005 – (Supporting role)
TEA PARTY – Dramafreak Productions – 2006 – (Featured role)
DUNWICH – Crawling Chaos Pictures – 2006 – (Featured role)
ALTERING CONCLUSIONS – Gold Shoe Productions – 2007 (Featured role)

STAGE

Numerous roles over the past 30 years for various theater groups,
both equity and non-equity. Some favorite roles include: Fagin in
OLIVER, Chief Bromden in CUCKOOS NEST, Scarecrow in WIZARD OF OZ,
Harry Rote in WAIT UNTIL DARK, Captain Hook in PETER PAN, Sidney
Bruhl in DEATHTRAP, and Scrooge in A CHRISTMAS CAROL.

OTHER
Founder/member of improvisational comedy group
E.J.Smackels

LINDA LEVEN

LINDA LEVEN

WWW.LINDALEVEN.COM

"UNIQUE, CHARISMATIC, A COMMANDING PRESENCE"

5' 8"   115 POUNDS   DARK AUBURN HAIR   HAZEL EYES

FILM:

" Loose Ends," Played: a telemarketer, Director: Peter Chan   "Hansel and Gretel: An Underground Fairy Tale", Played: the Witch, Director: Eduardo Ruano   "Cycles", Played: The Crone, Director: Carlos Caballero "Prime Season", Played: Madame-X, Director: Naoya Watanabe   "The Flesh Machine", Played: the boss, Director: Daniel Abella   "Prelude", Played: Innkeeper/Asylum nurse, Director: Richard Grassmann "Khameleon", Played: Khameleon, the strange Gothic woman, Director: Carol Ugbechie   "Untitled Short Animation", Voice-over: the old Hollywood actress, Director: Gladys Bensimon   "Mill Wheel", Played: Drunken mother, Cabaret Dancer, Director: Andrea Slavici   "(Ab) Used", Played: The Dream Vision, Director: Sofian Khan   "Last Minute Dating", Played: The D.J., Director: David Drach   "Exhibit 42", Played: Max's mother, Director: Glen Komsky   "Dead End Massacre", Played: Crazy Pam, Director: Scott Goldberg "Rubadub Documentary", Played: Storyteller, Director: Lars Haga   "Undertaker's Dozen", Played: Tina, Electra's friend, Director: T. Walker Price   "Deal With the D.E.V.I.L.", Played: Faust's Mother, Director: Miguel Rivera   "The Prank", Played: Provocative Woman, Director: Lorrie Bollard   "Free Loading", Played: Interviewer, Director: Tyler Greco   "Ingénue Blue", Played: Sable Kahn, actress, Director: Joseph Navarone "Untitled Work", Played: nurse/mother, Director: Vikash Nowlakha   "Host"(SciFi), Played: Chelsea – citizen undergoing parasitic socializing, Director: Nat Johnson   "Three Nocturnes", Played: an actress, Director: Alexis Raskin   "Deprivation", Played: the street prostitute, Director: Jessie Scolaro   "The Game's Afoot", Played: Fordyce Vanderbuilt, Director: Sal Iannaci   "The Laverne Affair", Played: the Servant, Director: Ramon Bloomberg   "Justin's Cage", Played: nurse, Director: Chino Moya   "Hotel Distortion", Played: woman with sugar obsession, Director: Robert Falls   "Contaxx", Played: cocktail waitress mother (lead), Director: Warren Bruttell   "747", Played: angry artist (lead), Director: Chino Moya   "The Quick Brown Fox", Played: Annabelle-head secretary, Director: Pete Levin   "Christ For a Buck", Played: conflicted mother, Director: Chris Cain   "Enzian and Tyrone", Played: the other woman, Director: Jay Chung   "Hide and Seek", Played: Aunt Sophie, Director: James M. Simak   "Welcome to Disneylandia", Played: TV show hostess, Director: Jose Fuentes   "Jane-The Story of a Young Stalker", Played: Monique-a friend, Director: Cybil Lake   "Fascination", Played: hostess of party of the dead, Director: Thomas Bukowski   "Yellow Light", Played: grandmother/storyteller, Director: Marshal Johnson   "Machines of Love and Hate ", Played: confessional lady (featured x), Director: Joe Parda   " 5 Days and … ", Played: Cherie-French mobster, Director: Eugene Efuni " Rien de Rien ", Played: strolling woman in red, Director: Aron Kantor   " I'll Bury You Tomorrow ", Played: Olive - morgue nurse, Director: Allen Kelly   " Man in Red ", Played: doctor's whore (featured x), Director: Gladys Bensimon   " First We Take Manhattan ", Played: sexy woman in bar, Director: Guy Frenkel   " Sign of the Times ", Played: older bitch model (featured x), Director: Tobias Fueter   " Material ", Played: Stacy, artist/murderess, Director: Alyson Richards   " Whatever Happened to Kathy? ", Played: Lilly, ex-actress, Director: Chris Cain   "Toxic Avenger 4 ", Offered role: mafia girl, Director: Lloyd Kaufman

T.V. and PUBLIC ART WORKS

"Dan Ackroyd Out There", Voice-over: Siris 6, Director: Wayne Novelli   The Dave Gold Show, Guest-Actress, Director: Dave Gold, Channel 57 – MNN   Pre-Pilot: "Friends Inside", Played: teacher, Producer: Jeff Simmons, Hallmark Entertainment   Documentary: "Islanders", Interviewee, Director: Emily Shepard   Commercial, ' ENVIWASH ' (laundry soap), Played: grandma (lead), Director: Csaba Bereczky   Sitcom, " The Sellouts ", Played: Chastity Purgis, abortion activist, Director: Rich Taylor   Talk Show, " Am I Nuts? ", Guest (1/2 hour) Channel 54, TALK AMERICA   "Untitled Dreaming Project, Played: floating body, Artist: David Solow   "The Influence Machine",(N.Y., London), Prose readings(lead), Artist: Tony Oursler

MODELING:

Modeled with photographers: John Fox, Anita Geraldo, G. Chin, Ken Lichtenwalter, Sacha Waldman Pictures exhibited: Photodistrict Gallery, Salmagundi Gallery, Neikrug Gallery, Libido Magazine, Klichten Web Gallery, Black Book Magazine (fashion), LIFE Magazine – 2000 (special edition), Baby Magazine(Paris).

DANCE: Pittsburgh Playhouse Ballet Company, Corps deBallet

FORMAL EDUCATION: M.A., NYU, Mathematics   B. A., NYU, Mathematics

Mike Marino

Mike Marino   SAG

(GIAA)
Guild Of Italian- American Actors

Hair: Black   Eyes: Brown   Height: 5'7"   Weight: 165 Lbs   Age: 27-32

TELEVISION:

Late Show With David Letterman	CBS / Reoccurring Role	Featured
Upright Citizens-Brigade	Comedy Central	Featured
Deadline	NBC	Featured
100 Center St.	A&E	Featured

FILM:

Devoured	Churchhill Productions, Tom Churchhill, Director	Supporting
Manhattanites	Loger Inc., Gregory Martin, Director	Featured
P.J.	P.J. Pictures LLC, Russell Emanuel, Director	Supporting
Across The Universe	Period Musical Inc., Julie Taymor, Director	Featured
Nikos The Impaler	Schnass Films GMBH, Andreas Schnass, Director	Featured
Cop Tales	Livingroom Theater Productions, Jason Morris, Director	Supporting
Sleepless Nights	Open Communications, Inc., William Hopkins, Director	Featured
Table One	Michael Bregman Productions, Bo Dietl, Director	Supporting
Fast Food, Fast Women	Fast Food, Fast Women Productions, Amos Kollek, Director	Supporting
The Bad Thing	Second Son Productions, Danny DeLorenzo, Director	Supporting
Big Apple	Big Apple Movie LLC, Dan Lerner, Director	Featured
Changing Lanes	Paramount Pictures, Michael John, Director	Featured
It Comes And Goes	First Step Productions, A.J. Yourish, Director	Lead/ Starring
The Meeting	Open Communications Inc./ Schnider Films, Blake Lawrence, Director	Supporting
The Big Day	Media Visions, Robert Andren, Director	Featured
XX/XY	XX/XY Productions, Austin Chick, Director	Featured
Pushing The Limit	Churchhill Productions, Tom Churchhill, Director	Supporting
The Contract	City Lights Entertainment, Domingo Martin, Director	Lead/ Starring

THEATRE:

Behold The Man	The Theatre Studio Inc., William Dean, Director	Lead/ Starring
Gotham Chronicle	Sanford Meisner Theatre, Nightforce Int'l Productions, Rod Barnes, Director	Supporting

TRAINING:

Monologue Technique	John Henry Richardson- Producer/ Director	Los Angeles
Audition Technique	Natalie Ford- Casting Director/ Acting Coach	Los Angeles
Master Class	Jeff Probst- Survivor Host and Writer/ Director of FINDERS FEE	Los Angeles

SKILLS:
New York State Drivers License
Write Poetry and Song Lyrics
Nun-Chucks/ Handball/ Air Hockey
Pierced Tongue/ Tattoo on back of head (Concealable)

Frank Garr

FRANK GARR

HAIR: silver   **EYES: lt. brown**   **HEIGHT: 5'8"**
WEIGHT: 160   **SHIRT: 15**   **WAIST: 34**
INSEAM: 28 ½   **SHOES: 9**   **SUIT/JACKET: 42**
AGE RANGE: 60's

FEATURE FILMS

Blazin Boys   pedestrian
19   pedestrian

TELEVISION

History Channel
Pantomine – singing, skits
1950's – 1970's

COMMERICAL/PRINT

Star Wars Promo
Howard Stern Promo
Channel Queens Public TV

WEBSITE/INTERNET

23/6   video with Jon Benjamin   23/6 Productions

THEATRE/PERFORMANCES

Musicals & songs: 1950's – 1970's

SPECIAL SKILLS

Comedy: stand-up, situation comedy, improvising
Singer: Popular
Dancing: modern, boogie, salsa, meringue
NYS Driver's License: auto/shift
Professional – Director USO: US Army and Europe

LANGUAGES

Fluent in Spanish
Fluent in Italian

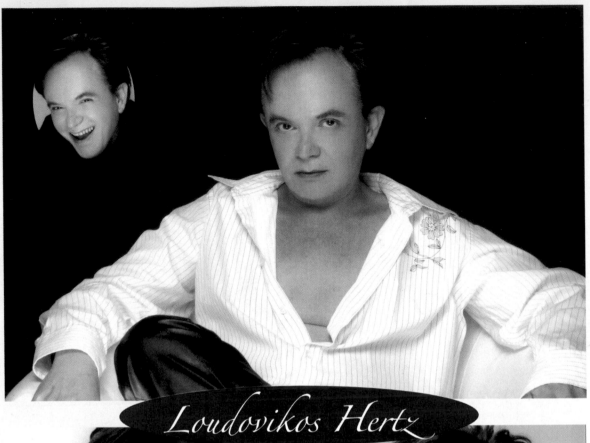

Loudovikos Hertz

From:Loudovikos Hertz

MY RESUME
I,m a Greek.I was born in Athens.My father an American citizen,had an import-export head-office with my mother in New York.I finished a Greek-
English high school in Piraeus and get a first in Classics I educated in Athens:School of Cinematography[3years course],licentiate:Costume designer,Awarded in Athens and London.7years I was cooperating with theatres in the process of plays.Literature of movies.Won a scholarship to Royal College of Art in London,
by Melina Merkouri[Minister of Greek Culture,in 80ties],studied Photographic Media [1year],underJ.W.Murphy,ATD,MSIAD.
I got into acting accidentally,through my studies.As a model worked in Art studio a Casting Director tested me on camera,gave me,my 1st secondary role
in a sciene fiction 'The Dragons of Eden',by Colin Goudie.Since then[1981]
I,d taken an active part such as a model in Art studios,cover of outbooks,folios by photographers,lifestyle:professional,Art nude,such as in melodramas,b-movies secondary roles and comedies in Greece without taste,which I,m looking for,sharp-set.
My favorite actresses are:Greta Garbo,Joan Crawford,Bette Davis,Meryl Streep,Nicole Kidman.
My favorite actors are:Edward G.Robinson,Douglas Fairbanks,JR.,William Holden,Lee Marvin,Robert De Niro,Al Pacino,George Clooney.
My favorite movies are:Ninotchka,Little Caesar,White Heat,Sunset Boulevard,What happened to Baby Jane?,Taxi Driver,Devil's Advocate,Sea of Love,Sophie's
Choise,The Good German,Goodnight and Goodluck,The Portrait,300 and 40's and 50's film noir.
My favorite writer is T.Williams.
My favorite movie's Costume designer is Edith Head.
Friendly with my best regards.Sincerely yours.Loudovikos.

211

Glen Adkins Jr.

Glen Adkins Jr.

FILM:

The Mandalorian Legacy*	Co-Star	Creative Group/Aaron Johnson

*in pre-production

TELEVISION:

Crisis Point	Co-Star	truTV/Adam Koster
Detective Privado	Guest Star	Azteca America/Alejandra Duque

COMMERCIALS:
Available on request

PRINT:

Solatube	Principal	Messina Design/Daniela Messina

MISCELLANEOUS:

House Taken	Co-Star	Lamon Jewett/Rodolfo Loyola
Youth Camp	Co-Star	Gloss Pictures/Ahmi Manson

TRAINING:

COLD READING	Nancy Friedman
SCENE STUDY	Nancy Friedman
AUDITION TECHNIQUE	Nancy Friedman
COMMERCIAL ACTING	John Sudol
Rehearsal Room	Carey Scott*

*newly enrolled

SPECIAL SKILLS:
Spanish: Read/Speak/Write (100% Fluent); 4-Time Marathon Finisher ; Licensed General Contractor; Certified Building Inspector; Airborne-Qualified Army Veteran; Dog Enthusiast, Songwriter; Karaoke Performer.

5'-9 ½"
200 lbs.
Green Eyes
Bald (Clean Shaven)

PHOTOGRAPHERS DIRECTORY INFO

A. Two Moons
917-309-6590
www.anthonytwomoons.com

a.m. photography
Autumn Marsilio
408-420-4990
autie1112@aol.com

Adventure Films Inc.
Photographer: Bob Williams
Office: 425-745-1057
Mobile: 206-351-9510

Babaldi Photography
333 W. 39th St., Suite 603
New York, NY 10018
212-253-8795
www.babaldi.com
mm@babaldi.com

Barry Burns Photography
260 W. 36th St., 2nd floor
New York, NY 10018
212-713-0103
www.barryburnsphotography.com
bb311photo@aol.com

Bradford Rogne Photography
Bradford Rogne
1308 Factory Pl., #512
Los Angeles, CA 90013
213-629-7488
www.PhotosLA.com
Info@PhotosLA.com

Brandin Photography
Photographer: Brandin Rackley
716 S. Orange Grove Ave.
Los Angeles, CA 90036
www.brandinphotography.com
brandinphotography@yahoo.com

Bryan Chin
276 West 20th Ave.
San Mateo, CA 94403
650-302-4985
www.deviouszen.sheezyart.com
jm.chin@yahoo.com

Burns Agency
John M. Burns
P.O. Box 10
Whitefield, NH 03824
603-479-1897
www.musicalnotesnmore.com
luchaburns@comcast.net

Daniel Gattas
freelancerdg@aol.com
danivenomous@myspace.com

Daniel W. Torres
www.danielwtorres.com

Dante Nassi for Barbizon
800-556-6335

David LaPorte Photography
310-452-4053
www.davidlaporte.com
davidlaporte@verizon.net

Dean Brewington
Seattle, WA
206-427-5416
www.artoffactfoto.com
dean@artoffactfoto.com

Desmond Duval
912-235-6880
bestphoto@yahoo.com

Douglas Gorenstein Studio
Douglas Gorenstein
315 W. 39th St., Suite 1308
New York, NY 10018
212-967-2810
www.DouglasGorenstein.com
douglas@douglasgorenstein.com

Fontana Studios
516-377-6565
fontstu@optonline.net

Foto Estudio California
Enrique Borja
2128 W. 7th St.
Los Angeles, CA 90057
Phone 213-387-5215

Gene Golden Photography
Gene Golden
818-882-9565
www.goldenvisart.com
goldenvisart@sbcglobal.net

Headshotsalive.com
Cile Bailey
111 Shaunell Dr.
Mandeville, LA 70448
985–264-1779
www.cile-bailey.com
cileartist@yahoo.com

Herman Stern
55 South Kukui Street, D2708
Honolulu, HI 96813
808-531-9930 or 808-220-6454

Hot Shot Photography Inc.
Eric Vardakis
1 Florida Park Dr. South, Suite 309
Palm Coast, FL 32137
386-445-7069
www.Hotshotphotographyinc.com
hotshotphotographyinc@gmail.com

J6Photo
Jason Colston
Arlington, VA
www.j6photo.com
jcolston6@gmail.com

James Deig
www.myspace.com/jimbostarrrr

James Brewster
432 Main St.
Sayreville, NJ 08872
732-698-2264
www.myspace.com/jimmybrewster
JamesLBrewster@aol.com

James Eakin
www.eakinphotography.com

Janene Otten
www.retna.com
desire_images@yahoo.com

Jeff Austin Photography
Jeff Austin
5102 Mill Pond Loop SE
Auburn, WA 98092
253-709-0464
www.jeffaustinphotography.com
austin.jeff@comcast.net
Years in business: 30

Jeff Howcroft
mkmiles27@aol.com

Joe Bowman Photography
Joe Bowman
Philadelphia, PA
215-545-5551
www.joebowmanphotography.com
bowman@joebowmanphotography.om

Jose Luis Pelaez
201–348-8008
Jose@pelaezproductions.com

Kendra Kracht
Crown Point, IN 46307
princesskendog@hotmail.com

Kim Karlen Photography
Kim Karlen
www.kimkarlen.com
info@kimkarlen.com

LC's Misfit Studios
www.lcmisfitstudios.com

Lance Lee
www.lindaleven.com

Landrum Creations Pro World Photography
Photographer: Dawn M. Landrum
1247 Norris Drive
Bossier City, LA 71111
318-742-6554
www.LandrumArtsLA.com
LandrumArt@aol.com

LaPorte Studio
John LaPorte
1610 Ludington St.
Escanaba, MI 49829
906-786-6653
www.laportestudio.com
laporte@chartermi.net

Leonard & Leonard Co.
Ushasi Kitchen
1825 Old New Bern Rd.
Chocowinity, NC 27817
252-916-2849
www.7194614.globaltravel.com
ushasibarua@aol.com

Lincoln Adler
www.lincolnadler.com

Marla L. Veal
Billings, MO
www.myspace.com/mlv_photography
mlv_photography@yahoo.com

Mary Ann Halpin Photography
323-874-8500
www.maryannhalpin.com
halpcro@aol.com

McClean Image Studio
James McClean
800 Ocala Rd., Suite 300–143
Tallahassee, FL 32304
850-339-5294 or +49-0151-50161515
www.McCleanImageStudio.com
James@McCleanImageStudio.com

Michael Dorn
www.frozenartphotography.com

Michael Evans Photography
Michael Evans
415-350-2602
www.d76.us
me@d76.us

Michele Marzano
432 Main St.
Sayreville, NJ 08872
732-698-2264
www.myspace.com/michelemarzano
Divamarzano@aol.com

Montana USA
LA: 323-521-8721
NY: 917-805-1871
www.montanausa.net
montanausa@gmail.com

N-Vision Photography
Melissa Bergerstock
Syracuse, New York
315-396-7288
www.nvisionphotography.com
melissa@nvisionphotography.com

N.E. Photo & Graphic Design
Israel Fishman
224 W. 30th St., Suite 707
New York, NY 10001
212-695-5030
www.nephotoanddesign.com

New Faces
516-822-4208

Nicole Standish
Greenwich, CT
203-637-2442
Nicolestandish@mac.com

Niels Johansen
Picture Time
133 NE 2nd Ave., #2811
Miami, FL 33132
954-554-2407
nj@picturetime.us
www.picturetime.us

Pan Takoulidis
Contact person: Judy
Arapaki 72
Athens, Kallithea 17676
011-30-210-9592282
Cell: 011-30-697-4884092
taktak@otenet.gr

Photographer Mark Ericksen
c/o Soundscapers
301 SE 5th St., #3
Minneapolis, MN 55414
612-861-9074
www.soundscapers.org
python@clermontlounge.com

PhotographerWillTravel.com
Edward M. Rollin
5131 William Penn Hwy.
Easton, PA 18045
Home: 610-438-0859
Mobile: 917-886-7500
www.PhotographerWillTravel.com
EdwardMRollin@aol.com

Photoworks Professional Lab
Contact person: Chris/David
2077-A Market St.
San Francisco, CA 94114
415-626-6800
www.Photoworkssf.com
chris@photoworkssf.com

Ray and Rita Normandeau
www.PostCardsR.us

Really Weird Productions
Contact person: R.W. Martin
3205 Big Hollow Rd.,
Starksboro, VT 05487
http://members.aol.com/H0LLYW00Dz
/index.html
VTActor007@aol.com

René Ojeda
718-919-1645

Riva Studios
Richard D. Trapani
5118 Kings Plaza Shopping Center
Brooklyn, NY 11234
718-692-2252
www.rivaphoto.com
rtrapani@juno.com

River Clark Photography
New York, NY
917-826-6271
www.riverclark.com
river@riverclark.com

Shama Ko Photography
Austin, TX
512-565-9014
www.skophoto.com

Sievers Photography
Dennis Sievers
11 W. Washington St., Suite 340
East Peoria, IL 61611
309-698-0800
www.sieversphoto.com
sieversphoto@ameritech.net

Stefanie Dadika
Tampa, FL
starrynight226@yahoo.com

Sunrise Studio
Daniel T. Lee
951-247-0706

Visions of You Photographs by Suzanne
Wall Township, NJ
732-681-7636
sbrand411@optonline.net

Zagari Photography
Lee Zagari
8400 Sunset Blvd.
West Hollywood, CA 90069
818-983-9034
www.ZagariPhotography.com
Lee@ZagariPhotography.com

ACTORS SHOT BY DIRECTORY

ACTORS	HEADSHOT
Adkins, Glen, Jr.	Lee Zagari, Zagari Photography
Bair, John D.	Corinne G. Bair
Bauer, Liz	Robert Hazzard
Begaye, Lyle	Lenora Begaye
Bennett, Sean	Maurizio Bacci, Babaldi Photography
Bey, Father Hannibal D. "Grand Master Priest Faustus"	Michael H. Bey
Breiner-Sanders, Melisa	Jason Colston
Brewster, James	Michele Marzano
Butt, Laura	Daniel Gattas
Burns, Carol	John M. Burns
Canady, Larry	Israel Fishman
Caul, Shayna "The Entertaina"	Jillian T. Weiss
Charett, DeAnna	Cile Bailey
Clark, Cindy	Brandin Rackley
Collins, Jason	Yvonne Witschard
Conroy, Maryellen	Carol Rosegg
Costello, Brian	LC's Misfit Studios
Coyle, Kevin	Visions of You Photographs by Suzanne
Cyphers, Leona	Richard D. Trapani
"D," Skippy	Skippy D (self portraits)
Dadika, Tony	Jose Luis Pelaez
Dale, Chester	Nicole Standish
DeFeis, Ray	Santa Bonsignore DeFeis
Deig, James	James Deig (self portrait)

ACTORS	HEADSHOT
Del Seamonds, Leeny	Justin Manteuffel for WonderlandTV.com
Denes, Nick	Melissa Bergerstock
Devery, Louise	Edward Morris Rollin
Dyer, Clement	Steven An and Jorge Borja
Ellis, Jamil O.	Sheldon Noland
Escritt, Jerrod	Dale Ausdemore
Estrada, Jade Esteban	Daniel W. Torres
Fagan, Ron	Dawn M. Landrum, Landrum Creations Pro
Falk, Steve	unknown
Ferniany, J. Michael	Elliot dePicciotto
Finlay, Jack	James McClean
Fishman, Renee "Philly"	Charles Beale
Frazier, Rita	Ray Normandeau
Gallagher, Orion	Geno Esponda
Garr, Frank	Israel Fishman
Gipson, Eric	James Eakin
Glatt, Kenneth	Jeff Austin
Goff, James "The Glow"	Stacey O'Hare
Granville, Hollis	Israel Fishman
Greeber, Mr.	Mark Ericksen
Hertz, Loudovikos	Pan Takoulidis
Horowitz, Seymour	unknown
Kaldor, Eric	unknown
Kendall, Jennifer	Autumn Marsillo
Kitchen, Ushasi	Leonard Martin
Krawchuk, Shelley	Herman Stern
Lam, Linda	Kim Karlen
Larson, Erin Douglas	Jeff Austin (Muscle and Hat Headshot), Bob Williams (suspenders headshot)
Leven, Linda	Lance Lee

ACTORS	HEADSHOT
Lombardi, Roberto	Joe Bowman
Lucas, John C.	Eric Vardakis, Hot Shot Photography
Lunser, Leo	Donald Twombley
Lyndon, Amy	Mary Ann Halpin
Marino, Mike	Janene Otten
Martin, R.W.	R.W. Martin (self portraits)
Marzano, Michele	James Brewster
Mason, Sabrina	Desmond Duval
Mayo, Stephen Andrew	Marla L. Veal
McGuire, Kit Carson	Shama Ko
Melbardis, Guntis	Dawn M. Landrum
Miles, Mindy	Jeff Honcroft
Morgan, Shelly	Jill Lederer
Narez, Chris	Dante Nassi
Nissen, Finch	Dawn M. Landrum
Normandeau, Ray	Rita Frazier
Paolini, Karen	Israel Fishman
Pasca, Joe	David LaPorte
Pires, David	Dennis Sievers
Presley, Sybil "The Tennessee Stress Buster"	Olan Mills
Reed, Willie "Big Dawg"	Dawn M. Landrum,
Rexx, Robert	Gene Holden
Reilly, Steve	Dean Brewington
Rodriguez, Johnnie	Michael Evans
Rollin, Edward Morris	Edward Morris Rollin (self portrait)
Russo, Joe	Kendra Kracht
Scott, John Henry	John Henry Scott (self portrait)
Seiden, Ray	Edward Morris Rollin
Sera, Kitten Kay	Montana USA
Shimunov, Nikolay	New Faces

ACTORS	HEADSHOT
Silfen, Jack "Cyclone"	Israel Fishman
Stauffer, Cindy	Michael Dorn
Strong, Robert	Lincoln Adler
Tevez, Oscar	René Ojeda
Thomas, Roxie	Lisa Katz
Thomson, Loretta	Daniel T. Lee
Tibbs, T. Boomer	Bernard Flanzraich
Timko, Susyn	Bradford Rogne
Traina, Pete	Frank Fontana, Fontana Studios
Tyler, Albert	Sears
Varick, Drew Rin	Dawn M. Landrum
Von Tilborg, Yenz	Niels Johansen
Walters, W.A.	Barry Burns
Wiegand, John	unknown
Welch, Rainey	River Clark
Wenzel, Mark	Barbara McLarney (Mime Headshot), David LaPorte (Smoking Jacket Headshot)
Wickowitz, Sheldon	Riva Studios
Witz, Rachel	A. Two Moons
Wu, Xingkai	Bryan Chin
Zawada, Jeff	John Laporte

ACTORS DIRECTORY

Adkins, Jr., Glen	gadkinsholyheadshot@gmail.com
Bair, John D.	jbairholyheadshot@gmail.com
Bauer, Liz	lbauerholyheadshot@gmail.com
Begaye, Lyle	lbegayeholyheadshot@gmail.com
Bennett, Sean	sbennettholyheadshot@gmail.com
Bey, Father Hannibal D. "Grand Master Priest Faustus"	hbeyholyheadshot@gmail.com
Breiner-Sanders, Melissa	mbreinersandersholyheadshot@gmail.com
Brewster, James	jbrewsterholyheadshot@gmail.com
Butt, Laura	lbuttholyheadshot@gmail.com
Burns, Carol	cburnsholyheadshot@gmail.com
Canady, Larry	lcanadyholyheadshot@gmail.com
Caul, Shayna "The Entertaina"	scaulholyheadshot@gmail.com
Charett, DeAnna	dcharettholyheadshot@gmail.com
Clark, Cindy	cclarkholyheadshot@gmail.com
Collins, Jason	jcollinsholyheadshot@gmail.com
Conroy, Maryellen	mconroyholyheadshot@gmail.com
Costello, Brian	bcostelloholyheadshot@gmail.com
Coyle, Kevin	kcoyleholyheadshot@gmail.com
Cyphers, Leona	lcyphersholyheadshot@gmail.com
"D," Skippy	skippydholyheadshot@gmail.com
Dadika, Tony	tdadikaholyheadshot@gmail.com
Dale, Chester	cdaleholyheadshot@gmail.com
DeFeis, Ray	rdefeisholyheadshot@gmail.com
Deig, James	jdeigholyheadshot@gmail.com
Del Seamonds, Leeny	ldelseamondsholyheadshot@gmail.com

Denes, Nick	ndenesholyheadshot@gmail.com
Devery, Louise	ldeveryholyheadshot@gmail.com
Dyer, Clement	cdyerholyheadshot@gmail.com
Ellis, Jamil O.	jellisholyheadshot@gmail.com
Escritt, Jerrod	jescrittholyheadshot@gmail.com
Estrada, Jade Esteban	jestradaholyheadshot@gmail.com
Fagan, Ron	rfaganholyheadshot@gmail.com
Falk, Steve	sfalkholyheadshot@gmail.com
Ferniany, J. Michael	mfernianyholyheadshot@gmail.com
Finlay, Jack	jfinlayholyheadshot@gmail.com
Fishman, Renee "Philly"	rsfishmanholyheadshot@gmail.com
Frazier, Rita	rfrazierholyheadshot@gmail.com
Gallagher, Orion	ogallagherholyheadshot@gmail.com
Garr, Frank	fgarrholyheadshot@gmail.com
Gipson, Eric	egipsonholyheadshot@gmail.com
Glatt, Kenneth	kglattholyheadshot@gmail.com
Goff, James "The Glow"	jgoffholyheadshot@gmail.com
Granville, Hollis	hgranvilleholyheadshot@gmail.com
Greeber, Mr.	greeberholyheadshot@gmail.com
Hertz, Loudovikos	lhertzholyheadshot@gmail.com
Horowitz, Seymour	shorowitzholyheadshot@gmail.com
Kaldor, Eric	ekaldorholyheadshot@gmail.com
Kendall, Jennifer	jkendallholyheadshot@gmail.com
Kitchen, Ushasi	ukitchenholyheadshot@gmail.com
Krawchuk, Shelley	skrawchukholyheadshot@gmail.com
Lam, Linda	llamholyheadshot@gmail.com
Larson, Erin Douglas	elarsonholyheadshot@gmail.com
Leven, Linda	llevenholyheadshot@gmail.com
Lombardi, Roberto	rlombardiholyheadshot@gmail.com
Lucas, John C.	jlucasholyheadshot@gmail.com
Lunser, Leo	llunserholyheadshot@gmail.com

Lyndon, Amy	alyndonholyheadshot@gmail.com
Marino, Mike	mmarinoholyheadshot@gmail.com
Martin, R.W.	rwmartinholyheadshot@gmail.com
Marzano, Michele	mmarzanoholyheadshot@gmail.com
Mason, Sabrina	smasonholyheadshot@gmail.com
Mayo, Stephen Andrew	smayoholyheadshot@gmail.com
McGuire, Kit Carson	kmcguireholyheadshot@gmail.com
Melbardis, Guntis	gmelbardisholyheadshot@gmail.com
Miles, Mindy	mmilesholyheadshot@gmail.com
Morgan, Shelly	smorganholyheadshot@gmail.com
Narez, Chris	cnarezholyheadshot@gmail.com
Nissen, Finch	fnissenholyheadshot@gmail.com
Normandeau, Ray	rnormandeauholyheadshot@gmail.com
Paolini, Karen	kpaoliniholyheadshot@gmail.com
Pasca, Joe	jpascaholyheadshot@gmail.com
Pires, David	dpiresholyheadshot@gmail.com
Presley, Sybil "The Tennessee Stress Buster"	spresleyholyheadshot@gmail.com
Reed, Willie "Big Dawg"	wreedholyheadshot@gmail.com
Reilly, Steve	sreillyholyheadshot@gmail.com
Rexx, Robert	holyheadshot@gmail.com
Rodriguez, Johnnie	jrodriguezholyheadshot@gmail.com
Rollin, Edward Morris	erollinholyheadshot@gmail.com
Russo, Joe	jrussoholyheadshot@gmail.com
Scott, John Henry	jscottholyheadshot@gmail.com
Seiden, Ray	rseidenholyheadshot@gmail.com
Sera, Kitten Kay	kseraholyheadshot@gmail.com
Shimunov, Nikolay	nshimunovholyheadshot@gmail.com
Silfen, Jack "Cyclone"	jsilfenholyheadshot@gmail.com
Stauffer, Cindy	cstaufferholyheadshot@gmail.com
Strong, Robert	rstrongholyheadshot@gmail.com
Tevez, Oscar	otevezholyheadshot@gmail.com

Thomas, Roxie	rthomasholyheadshot@gmail.com
Thomson, Loretta	lthomsonholyheadshot@gmail.com
Tibbs, T. Boomer	tbtibbsholyheadshot@gmail.com
Timko, Susyn	stimkoholyheadshot@gmail.com
Traina, Pete	ptrainaholyheadshot@gmail.com
Tyler, Albert	atylerholyheadshot@gmail.com
Varick, Drew Rin	drvarickholyheadshot@gmail.com
Von Tilborg, Yenz	yvontilborgholyheadshot@gmail.com
Walters, W.A.	wawaltersholyheadshot@gmail.com
Weigand, John	jweigandholyheadshot@gmail.com
Welch, Rainey	rwelchholyheadshot@gmail.com
Wenzel, Mark	mwenzelholyheadshot@gmail.com
Wickowitz, Sheldon	swickowitzholyheadshot@gmail.com
Witz, Rachel	rwitzholyheadshot@gmail.com
Wu, Xingkai	xwuholyheadshot@gmail.com
Zawada, Jeff	jzawadaholyheadshot@gmail.com

ACKNOWLEDGMENTS

We have to start by sincerely thanking every person who took the time to send us their headshots and résumés. And a big thanks as well to all the photographers who made this book possible. Without you, this book would be titled *Holy!* and would be full of blank pages. We wish all of you the best and hope that you make it in every way possible.

David Cross stepped up to the plate and definitely hit a double down the right field line that brought in two runs to give our book the lead in the eighth inning. David, you are our David Ortiz *and* our Jonathan Papelbon. May you never die!

We also owe a serious debt of gratitude to those casting directors and entertainment executives who so kindly opened their filing cabinets and allowed us to finger through their cache of headshots. In particular we'd like to thank Cecelia Pleva, Janine Michael, Anne Harris, Alison Cohn, Jennifer Rudin, Cristina F. Fowler, and Krissy Benge.

We consider ourselves blessed to have Kuhn Projects in our corner. Our agent David Kuhn believed in this project from the moment he saw it, and we couldn't be more appreciative of all the magic he has worked on our behalf. And we tip our hats to the unflappable Billy Kingsland, the Tim Gunn of literary agenting. Thanks also to Gerard Bradford.

Many thanks to the following folks, who gave us invaluable guidance and advice at various points along the way: John Hodgman, Amy Nickin, Matt Hall, Jon Glaser, Nick Caruso, Michael Kraft, Paul Hanson, Kevin Salwen, and Jonathan Margolis.

We are endlessly indebted to our editor, Kerri Kolen, who "got" the book from the get go. Her positivity, keen sense of humor, and guidance throughout this whole process were essential to the success of this book. Kerri, collaborating with you was effortless and a blast. We immediately felt like we were working with a friend, and now it's great to call you one.

David Rosenthal, thank you for saying "Yes" to our book. Your sage advice and wry sense of humor made us feel like we were at a comedy show and not at a publishing house. If we ever need to borrow a cat, we know who to go to.

To the rest of the team at Simon & Schuster—Aileen Boyle, Deb Darrock, Nina Schwartz, Victoria Meyer, Tracey Guest, Brian Ulicky, Leah Wasielewski, Jaime Putorti, Nancy Singer, Jackie Seow, and Michael Accordino—thanks to all of you for putting in so much work and effort. We appreciate each and every one of you.

FROM PATRICK

I want to thank, again and again and again, all the folks in this book, and that includes the photographers.

To my whip-smart wife, Cassie. You are my favorite editor. (Kerri, you're second, for sure.) I cannot thank you enough for all your support, guidance, and advice. You are like Tina Fey, Murphy Brown, and a liberal David Brooks rolled into one great woman.

From day one, Douglas brought a boundless energy, enthusiasm, and flow of great ideas to this project that made working on the book not only possible but enjoyable. I couldn't have asked for a better co-author.

Thanks to Tucker Voorhees at Principato Young Management for all your guidance through the years. I'm a fan of your comedy.

I want to thank my parents, Suzanne and Jerry, and the whole Borelli family for all their support through the years. And to Ellen and my new family in Madison—thanks for being so welcoming (that includes you, Harriet).

Eloise, you are my favorite dog in the whole world.

FROM DOUGLAS

I am deeply grateful to the actors and photographers who turned the vision of this project into the reality of this book.

To the multitalented Patrick Borelli, I couldn't have asked for a more awesome collaborator both on and off the ice. Your inspired ideas, work ethic, and sense of fun are a gift. Working with you on this common pursuit was as exhilarating as winning that local hockey championship. (Go Sled Dogs!)

Thank you to my amazing and inspirational wife, Sarah, for collaborating on the book of life, for letting me buy you hockey skates for Hanukkah, and for giving birth to our "rock star" son, Max ("Put down the camera, Daddy!")

To my family, extended family across the pond, dedicated friends who feel like family, and the Baum Group who are family, I appreciate your support in seeing this project hit the presses.

Thanks to the agents and casting directors who never took an interest in me as an actor, which led me to a successful career as a headshot photographer. Had it not been for your doors slamming shut in my face, the pages of this book would never have opened. Although, from time to time I still wonder . . . "Was it my headshot?"

FINAL THANK YOU

Finally, we would like to say that as we've gotten to know the actors in *Holy Headshot!*, we've been struck by their love of acting, moving personal stories, and intense desire for success and fame. In turn, we've become their biggest fans. We wish them the greatest success in achieving their dreams. It is our hope that being included in this book will somehow help to open doors and lead to the day when we hear them proclaim, "It's an honor just to be nominated."

—Patrick and Douglas

ABOUT THE AUTHORS

PATRICK BORELLI is a comedian and writer living in Brooklyn. His writing has appeared in *McSweeney's Quarterly* and *The Onion*. He's been a staff writer for *Cheap Seats* (ESPN Classics) and *Assy McGee* (Cartoon Network's Adult Swim). He is the co-creator of *Thunderpoint*, an animated series for SuperDeluxe.com. He's also written freelance for *Triumph the Insult Comic Dog*. His performance credits include appearances on Comedy Central's *Premium Blend*, *Late Night with Conan O'Brien*, VH1's *Best Week Ever*, the Cartoon Network's *Home Movies* and *Assy McGee*, and Public Radio's *Fair Game*.

www.patrickborelli.com

DOUGLAS GORENSTEIN is an acclaimed headshot photographer with clients appearing on Broadway, television, and in feature films. He teaches headshot seminars at many leading acting programs. Photographic assignments include performances by Meryl Streep, Jennifer Lopez, and the cast of *The Jersey Boys*. He has photographed Mayor Michael Bloomberg, fashion designer Kay Unger, and attorney Barry Scheck. His work has appeared in *Variety*, *The Dramatist*, *Backstage*, and *Global Rhythm*. As an actor he has appeared on *Late Night with Conan O'Brien*, in *The Brothers Karamazov* for the Lincoln Center Directors Lab, and *University* directed by Gene Hackman. He is a member of the Actors Studio, where he wrote and performed "The Impersonation." Currently he is developing several television and book projects with Mr. Borelli. He lives with his wife and son in New York City.

www.douglasgorenstein.com